A
BIRD'S-EYE
VIEW
OF
JAPAN

© by Japan Travel Bureau, Inc.
ALL RIGHTS RESERVED
ISBN 0-87040-375-3
First Edition 1976
Second Edition 1978

The photos in this book, with
the exception of those taken by
the Japan Travel Bureau, Inc. are
reproduced through the courtesy
of the Japan National Tourist
Organization.

Printed in Japan

Yellow-tinged leaves at Sanzen-in Temple in the outskirt of Kyoto.

"Kamakura," a pleasant festival for children of the snow country.

7-5-3 festival.

"Hina matsuri" or doll's festival.

Acrobatic New Year's parade of fireman.

Traditional sumo tournament.

A scene of "hanami" at the site of Hirosaki Castle

Mt. Fuji with its mirror image on the surface of Lake Kawaguchi.

CONTENTS

PREFACE

In this modern, speed-oriented age of ours when the world changes so rapidly that it's difficult to keep pace, visitors to Japan's shores may be surprised to find so many things that actually remained unchanged.

In their quest for "Old Japan" or the "Real Japan," visitors may tend to overlook the older aspects of the country since more often than not the old stands side-by-side with the new. But once discovered it is this unique blend of the old with the new that fascinates so many foreign tourists.

"A Bird's-Eye View of Japan" is specifically designed to open your eyes to the many wonders you are bound to come across during your travels around Japan. A sort of Encyclopedia Japonica, it contains a hundred and one things Japanese, from enchanting scenery and wondrous works of art to quaint social customs and exotic patterns of life, some unchanged for centuries.

Since this guide was especially published in a handy pocket-size, it is earnestly hoped that you will find it interesting and informative enough to refer to "A Bird's-Eye View of Japan" from time to time during your visit to our country.

THE EDITOR

Tokyo
April 1979

NOTES

1. All names of Japanese people are given in Western manner, ie., the surname after the given name.
2. For weights and measures, the metric system is used.
3. The following abbreviations are used in the text:

alt. = altitude	m. = meter(s)
Bldg. = Building	min. = minute(s)
c. = centigrade	mm. = millimeter(s)
cm. = centimeter(s)	Mt. = Mountain, Mount
ha. = hectare(s)	Mts. = Mountains
hr(s). = hour(s)	(Mountain Range)
kg. = kilogram(s)	pop. = population
km. = kilometer(s)	R. = River
lit. = literally	

LAND AND THE PEOPLE

Emperor

Ancestor   It has been said that the initial ancestor of the present Emperor Hirohito was Emperor Jimmu, or Hatsu-kunishirasu Sumeramikoto—the first leader of the Yamato Court. The court was one of the most influential family groups controlling the State. Emperor Jimmu is said to have ascended the throne as the first emperor in 660 B.C., although the authenticity of these points is still being debated by historians.

It was true that until well before World War II, quite a few people added 660 years to the calendar year and called it "kigen," or origin of the State. According to their calculation, the year 1979 would become "kigen 2639."

Hirohito is Japan's present 124th emperor.

History The period during which emperors exercised political power lasted until the latter part of the 12th century. When the emperor appointed Yoritomo Minamoto, a samurai (warrior), as "Sei-i-Taishogun" (or shogun for short, meaning generalissimo for subjugation of the eastern barbarians), political control remained in the hands of the "samurai" until the Meiji Restoration in 1868. During this period, the official capital was Kyoto, but the samurai's government capital was set up in Kamakura (by Yoritomo) and later moved to Edo (present-day Tokyo) by the eventual successors—the Tokugawas. In 1868, actual political control was returned to the emperor. Edo Castle, where the "shogun" had resided was renamed the Imperial Palace.

Imperial Family Emperor Hirohito became a symbol of the State under the postwar Constitution in which sovereignty rests with the people.

Hirohito was born on April 29, 1901 and ascended the throne in 1926. For 18 days starting on September 29, 1971, the emperor made a tour of Europe, visiting seven countries. On September 30, 1975, the emperor began a 14-day visit to the United States of America. These two visits marked the only times he has left Japan as emperor. The emperor is deeply versed in biology, especially marine biology and botany, and has written a number of books on these sciences.

Empress Nagako was born in the Family of Kuni (former branch of the Imperial Family). The empress is skilled in Japanese painting among other things.

Crown Prince Akihito is interested in sports, including tennis, horseback riding, skiing and swimming. In

April 1959, Akihito married Michiko Shoda, a commoner. It is said that they met by chance on the tennis courts. They have two sons and a daughter.

National Flag of Japan

"Hinomaru no hata" or "nisshoki," standing for "the flag of the rising sun with a white background," was officially proclaimed the national flag in 1870. The flag is rectangularly shaped with a length-width proportion of 10–7. The red sun, set in the center, has a diameter measuring three-fifths of the width.

National Anthem

The national anthem of Japan is commonly called "Kimigayo," which means "to celebrate my lord's dynasty." The lyrics were taken from a poem written by an unknown poet. The melody was composed by Hiromori Hayashi, a musician of the former Imperial Household Agency and it was played first in 1880.

The anthem was always played at national or public events before World War II, but this is not always the case today. The Japan Sumo Association traditionally plays the national anthem on the last day of sumo tournaments. As a result, many young people think "Kimigayo" is music for a closing ceremony without realizing it is the national anthem.

Salaried Men

"Salary Man"   White-collar workers are called in Japanized English "salary man," a term representing both singular and plural forms. "Salary man" can easily be identified by their appearance: neatly cropped hair, a suit of subdued color with a white shirt (although colored and striped shirts have been on the increase recently) and tie. This attire is

"Salary man"

regarded almost as a uniform for salaried men, who now total about 36 million.

Loyalty to the company is usually high, although the generation gap diversifies the degree of their loyalty.

"Nenko Joretsu" Once a person (including those employed in managerial positions) is employed in Japan, his salary increases year after year on the basis of the seniority system. Japanese management generally believes that the ability and contribution yielded by an employee is reinforced with each succeeding year that he works. Japanese management, both public and private, usually considers it is best to stick to the seniority system in acquiring labor and in keeping it in a stable condition. Such a system is called "nenko joretsu"—literally "the year's order" or "by order of the year." For an employee, it is like riding an escalator: one may not advance two or more steps upward when someone ahead of him is riding on the very next.

Lifetime Employment   The hiring of workers on the basis of lifetime contract is one of the special characteristics of the Japanese enterprise and governmental system. Strictly speaking, they work until reaching retirement age, which ranges from 55 to 60 years of age, depending on the type of enterprise. Government organizations and a few enterprises have an unlimited retirement age.

When retirement age arrives, employees usually receive their severance in one lump sum, averaging 15 million yen per person. This is followed by a national pension or a pension worked out by the company, or both.

Salary   The average income of a salaried man is ¥3,100,000 a year. The breakdown included his basic salary (occupying the major portion) plus allowances for dependents, transportation expenses, etc. In addition to his monthly salary, he receives two or three bonuses a year. The bonus, the amount of which is negotiated through collective bargaining, is usually paid to employees in June and December. Some companies pay extra bonus when the company closes its fiscal balance sheet in a more favorable condition than its income budget.

Labor Unions

Labor Unions   The right of workers to organize and carry out collective bargaining is protected by the Trade Union Law. Japanese trade unionism is characterized by separate company unions, the membership of each union being limited to the workers employed by that company. This is in contrast to the horizontal organization of unions in other countries.

There are about 59,000 labor unions with a total membership of some 12 million. Most of these members also belong to one of the big union federations—Sohyo (General Council of Trade Unions of Japan), Domei (Japan Confederation of Labor), Shinsambetsu (National Federation of Industrial Organizations) and Churitsuroren (Federation of Independent Unions). They differ from each other primarily in tactics and political coloring.

"Shunto"   Workers usually manage to have their salaries raised every year, with the wage-hike movement beginning in April to coincide with the first month of Japan's fiscal year. The collective bargaining, in most cases, takes a certain amount of time before mutual agreement is reached. To pressure management, workers often stage a walkout. Since this phenomenon is seen throughout Japan in the spring, it is called "shunto"—literally, spring struggle.

"Jumpo Toso" or Work to Rule Struggle   In lieu of a strike, JNR employees often slow down the speed of their trains resorting to "jumpo" (work to rule)—a type of slowdown tactics.

Why is the slowdown called "work to rule struggle?" The answer will be found in the following description:

Years ago, JNR began using a mechanical system called ATS (Automatic Train Stop System), which automatically warns train drivers when trains require operational stops. The driving rule calls for the train engineer to follow the instructions given by the ATS.

In the busy hours, however, trains actually run at higher speed than the ATS standards to cope with the demand for operating trains at two-minute intervals during the rush hours. During the hours, it is up to the judgment of the drivers rather than that of the ATS to operate the trains.

When things get sticky in collective bargaining, JNR employees often cling to this rule and painstakingly double check the ATS, slowing down trains, throwing schedules into confusion and causing huge crowds of waiting passengers at railway stations.

Agriculture

The farming population decreased from 27 million in 1955 to 23 million today despite a 12.17 percent increase in the national population during the same period. This means that farmers have been pouring into other fields such as mining, construction, manufacturing, transportation and the service industry.

"Sanchan," (a collective way of calling three family members: mother—"kaachan," grandfather—"jiichan" and grandmother—"baachan") are said to be the only ones still left on the farm. However, a gradual turnabout in the movement of the population is believed to have taken place immediately after the end of the high economic growth period in 1972.

Population

Japan has a total population of 112,145,133 according to a census taken by the Ministry of Home Affairs. In terms of age groupings, the population of children is 27 million, the adult population (15 to 59 years) comes to 71 million and the population of the aged (60 years or over) totals 12 million as of 1976. In 1977, the average life expectancy is 72.69 years for males and 77.95 years for females.

It is estimated that by 2025 Japan will have a population of 140,000,000 with the number of aged people exceeding 31 million thus accounting for the highest percentage in the total.

Abortion

Abortion is permitted in Japan if it is considered that the mother's health is endangered based on medical or economic reasons, under the Eugenic Protection Law enacted in 1948. A recent newspaper survey showed that one out of three married women under 50 years of age has had at least one abortion.

It is estimated that about 13,000 doctors are licensed to perform abortions. A report by doctors gives the number of abortions performed in 1975 as 700,000.

Pensions

A worker employed by a company may receive about ¥1,200,000 a year from the age of 55 or 60 (usually considered as the retirement age) provided he has no job and has regularly paid the pension fees (about ¥8,200 a month; for 25 years or more.

The national pension fee required is ¥2,200 a month, and the period of payment is for 25 years or more. The amount of pension one is entitled to receive a year is calculated by multiplying ¥1,300 by the number of months he has paid his fees. He receives the pension from the age of 65, if he is not engaged in any jobs.

Geographical Position

Japan extends 2,790 km., from lat. 45°33′N to lat. 20°25′N. It includes four major islands: Hokkaido (83,511 sq. km.), Honshu—the main island (230,841 sq. km.), Shikoku (18,789 sq. km.) and Kyushu (44,296 sq. km.) plus thousands of smaller islands to comprise a total area of 377,435 sq. km.

Japan is about 1.5 times as large as the United Kingdom and $\frac{1}{25}$ as large as the United States.

Japan's coastline extends for 26,505 km., including

bays, bights and inlets, all of which add greatly to the unique nature of its landscape.

"Sakura Zensen" or the Cherry-blossom Front

Cherry trees begin bursting into bloom as the first spring waves of warm air wash over Japan. The first blossoms are naturally seen in the southern part of Japan, thence day by day move northward.

Since cherry blossoms are at their best only for a couple of days, the Meteorological Agency announces the estimated cherry-blossom time for each area by the daily plotting of a line on a map. This line is called "sakura zensen," or the cherry-blossom front.

5.15
5.5
4.25
Cherry-blossom
front
4.15
4.5
3.25

"Bai-U"

"Bai-u," or rainy season starts around June 10 and ends about July 15. It is commonly called "bai-u" (lit. plum and rain); in other words, it rains at the same time that plum trees bear their fruit. The rainy season is also called "tsuyu" which means "dew" since rain at this time of year falls as gently as the dew.

Typhoons

The time when the God of Wind does most of his huffing and puffing on Japan is from the end of August to mid-September. Although typhoons are generally unwelcome because of the chaos they cause, at least they provide up to about 25 percent of the year's rainfall and ensure

21

bumper rice crops in autumn.

A chemical experiment aimed at calming typhoons by splitting silver iodide is still in its infant stage.

Composition of Land Space

Japan has a total land space of 377,435 sq. km., of which about 60,000 sq. km. is devoted to agricultural use and 260,000 sq. km. is covered by forests. Another 5,500 sq. km. consists of plains, 11,000 sq. km. is occupied by rivers, canals, lakes and ponds, 10,000 sq. km. is taken up by various structures, 6,900 sq. km. is set aside for roads and the remaining 24,000 odd sq. km. is covered by miscellaneous smaller items.

Housing

Housing Problem   The housing shortage is regarded as one of the social problems in Japan. Although increased construction costs are partly responsible, high land prices are largely to blame.

In Tokyo, for instance, more than 3.7 million households (one-third of the capital's population) need private houses. They are currently living in apartments consisting of two living rooms plus a kitchen, which rent for around ¥40,000 a month. Private houses (mostly "built-for-sale" types) cost 15–25 million yen. Although one can take advantage of the housing loan system through the Housing Loan Corporation and city banks, it takes almost 20 years for a debtor to repay the loan. Rates for a housing loan are 8.4% for 1–5 years, 8.7% for 6–10 years and 9% for 11–20 years by banks (rates differ slightly depending on banks), and 5% by the Housing Loan Corporation. Needless to say, applications to the latter are at a premium.

Land Prices   For years, land prices have been skyrocketing but in 1975 they began calming, levelling off, even declining to some extent. The land price in Japan is sometimes calculated on the basis of a unit called "tsubo" measuring 3.3 sq. m. The highest land price is at Shinjuku 3-chome in Tokyo and costs ¥14.1 million per "tsubo." Next comes a piece of real estate at Ginza 5-chome, also in Tokyo, priced at ¥13.5 million per "tsubo."

Here are the average land prices per "tsubo" in three largest cities: ¥500,000 in Tokyo, ¥300,000 in Osaka, ¥200,000 in Nagoya.

"Danchi" To cope with the heavy demand for housing, the Japan Housing Corporation was established in 1955. The corporation has concentrated on building large blocks of apartments, or flats called "danchi." As of 1976, there are 1,230 "danchi" consisting of 978,000 apartments built by the corporation. Each flat has two living/bedrooms (sometimes more), a dinette called "dining-kitchen" and a bathroom.

"Mansion" A condominium is called a "mansion" in Japan. Each apartment generally has two, three or more living/bedrooms usually larger than those offered by the Japan Housing Corporation, a dinette and a bathroom. Dwellers are charged an administrative maintenance fee ranging ¥7,000 to ¥50,000 a month. Because of its high-rise structure, new condominium construction projects invariably raise problems with the neighbors over blocking their sunlight and disturbing their television reception.

Nuclear Family

A recent trend shows that young couples especially after their marriage, are unlikely to live with their parents, partly because of the generation gap and partly because of inadequate housing conditions.

Although the average family numbered only 3.69

members in 1970, the National Land Agency predicts that the size of family will decrease even further to 3.25 by 1980.

Tokaido Megalopolis

On the Pacific coast of Japan's main island of Honshu between Tokyo (pop. 11,370,000) and Osaka (pop. 2,650,000) lies the nation's fourth largest city of Nagoya (pop. 2,070,000), 366 km. southwest of Tokyo. This coastal section constitutes the most densely populated area in Japan and is often called the "Tokaido megalopolis." One of the main reasons for constructing the Tokaido Shinkansen Line was to ease the jammed-up traffic situation that existed in this area. Urban problems—housing, intra-city traffic, poverty and pollution—plague the area, as the population of this megalopolis keeps growing year after year.

"Danchi"

PLACES
OF INTEREST

Lake Akan

Lake Akan is the main attraction of the Akan National
Park in Hokkaido. Situated between the two peaks of
Me-Akan and O-Akan, it is a caldera lake 22.5 km. in
circumference and 36.6 m. deep. This lake is particularly
noted for its unique ball-like green weed called "marimo,"
a species of weed found only in a few lakes in Japan. Since
its world-wide distribution is extremely limited, it is under
the protection of the government as a "Special Natural
Monument." Visitors to the lake can view the "marimo"
from the sightseeing boat that makes a tour of the lake.

Lake Mashu

Lake Mashu in the Akan National Park is often called the "lake of mystery" because of the mysterious atmosphere surrounding it and the nearby area. Its deep blue water is transparent as far down as 42 m. On its east side soars Mt. Kamui-Nupuri with its strange shape. The sheer cliffs of the lake, about 200 m. high, are so steep that no one can reach the water's edge. The fact that there are no outlets from the lake also adds to the mystery. Since the lake is often covered with mist, visitors are sometimes unable to view the entire lake.

Noboribetsu

Noboribetsu is one of the most popular spa resorts in Hokkaido, visited by most tourists traveling through this part of the country. Its thermal water is said to be efficacious in the treatment of various ailments. The Daiichi-Takimoto Ryokan, one of the oldest inns there, offers "Sen-nin-buro" (lit. 1,000-man bath), consisting of 40 pools and containing a variety of thermal waters.

"Showa Shinzan"

"Showa Shinzan" (lit. new mountain of Showa), rising just on the southern shore of Lake Toya, is an entirely new mountain formed in September 1946. People living in the area felt earthquakes more than 100 times in late 1943 and found the land around there had risen to a height of more than 50 m. After repeated eruptions, the earth rose gradually until it reached a height of 408 m. in 1946. The new mountain topped with lava is still steaming at several points.

Osore-Zan

Osore-zan (lit. terrible mountain) rises at the center of Shimokita Peninsula at the northern tip of Honshu (the largest of Japan's four main islands). It consists of eight peaks, which embrace two crater lakes—Lake Usori and Lake Kamafushi. On the northern shore of Lake Usori is Osore-zan Spa. There are also many geysers and fumaroles called "hells" in the caldera of the mountain.

Mt. Osore-zan has long been regarded as a holy mountain of the district. It was explored in the 9th century by Jikaku-Daishi, a noted priest of the time who founded the Bodaiji Temple on the northern shore of the present Lake Usori. A shaman, who supposedly can relay the words of the dead, is said to appear at the temple at the annual festival in July.

Matsushima

Matsushima (lit. pine-clad island), about 20 km. to the east of Sendai in Miyagi Prefecture, is famous as one of the "Scenic Trio of Japan." Matsushima is composed of numerous isles dotting Matsushima Bay. Varying in size and shape, most of them are covered with green pines. There are many historic buildings along Matsushima Bay, including Godaido Temple, Zuiganji Temple and Kanrantei—all dating back to the 16th century. The latter was a villa of the provincial lord Masamune Date.

Goshikinuma

Goshikinuma (lit. five-colored lakes) is a collective name for more than 200 lakes and tarns dotting the Bandai Plateau in the northern part of Fukushima Prefecture. Goshikinuma is one of the chief attractions of the Bandai-Asahi National Park that also includes the Bandai Plateau. Many of the lakes here have verdant isles that enhance the beauty of the scenery. Goshikinuma is so named because the lakes differ from each other in color. According to scientific proof, the oxidized rocks in the lake color the water various hues, depending on the depth of the water and the brightness of the sun.

Asakusa

Asakusa in Tokyo has long been famous for its Sensoji Temple, which is popularly known by the name of the Asakusa Kannon (Goddess of Mercy).

The red-painted Kaminarimon Gate of the Sensoji Temple is the landmark of the area. The approach to the main temple building leading up from the Kaminarimon Gate is called "Nakamise" Street, where cakes, toys, clothing, folkcraft goods and other fancy articles are for sale.

Adding to the attractions of the temple is a five-story pagoda. Reconstructed in 1973, it is 57 m. high and stands on a 4 m. high base. In the temple grounds is the Asakusa Shrine.

All in all, Asakusa is famous as an area that still retains the atmosphere of the old Edo days (1603–1867).

Ameyoko Street

Ameyoko Street in Ueno, Tokyo, is a "mecca" for shoppers. People throng to this part of the city all day long, browsing for good buys. The street extends between the JNR Yamanote Line and Hirokoji Avenue—the main thoroughfare of the Ueno area. Ameyoko Street is a veritable beehive of small, narrow passages. This section now sells not only various kinds of foodstuffs and daily necessities, but also imported articles ranging from perfumes to golf clubs—all prices far cheaper than can be found at any other place in the city.

Akihabara Street

Akihabara Street in Tokyo is noted for its large cluster of shops and stores handling electric appliances. There are more than a hundred shops that specialize in electric appliances.

All kinds of electric products are on sale, ranging from color television sets, radios, refrigerators, washing machines and micro wave ranges to stereo equipment and components. The shops are conveniently concentrated in the area around Akihabara Station on the JNR Yamanote Line.

Because everything is sold at a discount of 20 percent or more, many people come here regularly to buy their household products. A shopping area similar to that at Akihabara is also located at Nippombashi in Osaka.

Shinjuku

Shinjuku, with four department stores and many fashionable shops, is one of the most popular shopping centers in the metropolis. The west-side area of Shinjuku Station has been rapidly developed in recent years under the "Shinjuku Sub-City Program." This part of the city is dominated by a group of skyscrapers, some rise as high as 225 m. The area around Shinjuku Station features a highly developed underground shopping center, consisting of many sections and spreading in all directions like a labyrinth.

Tama Zoological Park

Tama Zoological Park is in Hino City, a part of the Tokyo Metropolis. It extends over a hill, covering an area of 3.3 ha. It contains about 16 species of animals collected from different parts of the world. Most of them roam free in an area separated from visitors by deep moats or high walls. As the animals wander about in the park much as they do in their own habitats, the visitors can watch them from the windows of the "Lion Bus," a motorcoach operated regularly by the park management.

"Kodomo-no-Kuni"

"Kodomo-no-kuni," or Children's Land, which is located in Yokohama's Kohoku Ward, is a pleasure and recreational park for children. The park spreads over a part of Tama-kyuryo (Tama Hills) and occupies an area of 97 ha. Built in 1965 in memory of the wedding of the Crown Prince and Princess, it is provided with many recreational facilities for children. There are also a driving school for children, a craft center where youngsters can make anything they want, a pasture with cows, sheep and goats, and a variety of other facilities.

"Minka-En"

"Minka-en," or village-house garden, in Kawasaki, Kanagawa Prefecture, is a unique park built for both educational and recreational purposes. It is really an open-air museum containing 17 old houses brought from the countryside in and around Kanagawa Prefecture and reassembled here.

People visiting them can learn about the way people lived more than 200 years ago. The "Minka-en" is laid out over a series of wooded hills, with each house placed in the natural setting in which it was originally built.

The Fuji-Five Lakes

The Fuji-Five Lakes district in Yamanashi Prefecture is nestled around the northern foot of Mt. Fuji. Because of its scenery, fresh air, good roads and many recreational facilities, the district is a delightful area for outings.

The five lakes are Yamanaka, Kawaguchi, Saiko, Shoji and Motosu in order of their location from east to west, all lying more than 700 m. above sea level. Lakes Kawaguchi and Yamanaka are especially popular because of the inverted image of Mt. Fuji mirrored upon the waters.

Daibutsu in Kamakura

The Daibutsu, or the Great Buddha of Kamakura, Kanagawa Prefecture, is one of the "must-see" attractions for the tourist. Kamakura flourished as the seat of the Kamakura Shogunate Government in the 12th to .14th century. The Daibutsu is an image of Amitabha cast in 1252 and measures 11.4 m. in height from its base.

The Daibutsu was formerly sheltered in a large wooden building, but it was washed away by tidal waves in 1495. Since then, the image of Buddha has remained in the open. The interior of the body can be inspected by offering a small donation; it is possible to reach its shoulders by a narrow stairway.

"Ninja-Dera"

"Ninja-dera" (lit. temple for masters of invisibility) is the popular name given to the Myoryuji Temple in Kanazawa City, Ishikawa Prefecture. Its main building has many secret rooms equipped with special devices peculiar to the art of invisibility and so designed that no one can sneak unawares into the building.

In the Edo period (1603–1867), the chief retainers of the provincial Lord Maeda often assembled at this temple, regarding it as one of their fortresses.

"Ninjutsu," or the art of invisibility, developed in early feudal days as a system for obtaining information on the secret plans and intentions of one's rivals.

"Edo-Mura"

"Edo-mura," or Edo village, is located at Yuwaku Spa on the outskirts of Kanazawa City. "Edo-mura" contains about 20 old houses and buildings—all built during the Edo period. Among the buildings on display here are the mansion of the councilor of the provincial lord Maeda, shops, farmhouses and the inn used exclusively by the "daimyo" (feudal lord). These structures were brought here and restored to their original state to show the way life

A farmhouse in "Edo-mura"

was lived in the Edo period.

"Meiji-Mura"

"Meiji-mura," or Meiji village, is a kind of an open-air museum which can be reached in about an hour by bus from Nagoya. The village features a collection of old buildings of the Meiji era (1868–1912) as well as a display of the folk materials used in those days. "Meiji-mura" includes the old St. John Church, the official residence of the principal of former Peer's School, a schoolroom of No. 4 High School, the Shinagawa Lighthouse, etc. An old steam locomotive and a streetcar used early in the Meiji era are also on exhibit in the village.

Nara Park

Nara Park is popularly called Deer Park by foreign visitors. It occupies the central part of Nara City and covers an area of 520 ha. This beautiful natural park is wooded with cedar and oak trees as well as wisteria vines. The tame deer, about 1,000 in number, roam free in the park and often approach visitors for food. They are called back to their pens by a horn blown when evening comes. It is customary for the deer in the park to have their horns trimmed on the day of the traditional Deer-horn Cutting Ceremony, annually observed in autumn.

"Takamatsu-Zuka"

"Takamatsu-zuka" is located in Asuka Village in Nara Prefecture, where the Asuka culture flourished in the 7th to 8th century. The tumulus, which was excavated in March 1972, is supposed to have been built in the 7th century. The unearthed objects from the tomb provide a revealing insight into the cultural life of the nobles of the 7th century. They customarily built gorgeously furnished and decorated tombs to display their power and prosperity.

The "Takamatsu-zuka" tumulus was constructed of stone in a cave-like style, and on the walls of the stone room are splendidly colored murals. The mound is rather small in size and round in shape, with a diameter of 18 m. Some ancient mirrors and bones of the dead were also unearthed from this mound.

Daibutsu in Nara

The Daibutsu, the Great Image of Buddha, in Nara is probably the largest of its kind in the world. It is housed in a large wooden structure, which is called the "Daibutsuden," or the hall of the Great Buddha. The Daibutsu belongs to the Todaiji Temple, founded in 752 by order of Emperor Shomu (701–756). The bronze image of Rushanabutsu, stands 16.2 m. high. This gigantic image of Buddha was completed in 749, but has been repaired since then in many places. The priests of the temple thoroughly clean the statue once a year by removing all the dust that collects on the body.

Horyuji Temple

The Horyuji Temple in Nara is located in the western suburbs of the city. It was founded in 607 by Prince Shotoku (573–621), regent of the Empress Regnant Suiko. Prince Shotoku was a great statesman of his time as well as a patron of Buddhism. The Kondo (Main Hall) of the temple is reputed to be one of the oldest wooden buildings in the world. Its 28 massive pillars are built in a style similar to Greek design, with a slight convex swelling in the lower shaft.

Other important structures of the Horyuji Temple are the Nandaimon Gate built in 1493, the five-story pagoda and the Yumedono, or Hall of Dreams.

Imai-Machi Town

Imai-machi Town, included within the city limits of Kashihara in Nara Prefecture, is characterized by the unique appearance of its streets, retaining the atmosphere of an Edo period (1603–1867) town. The streets of the town cross each other like a checker board and are extremely narrow. Most of them are lined with rows of old-fashioned houses standing side by side. Imai-machi is one of those rare places in Japan where one can see old Edo and Meiji period houses grouped together.

Dreamland in Nara

The Dreamland Amusement Centers in Nara and Yoko-hama are modeled after Disneyland in the U.S. The one in Nara is located on the outskirts of the city and can be reached in 20 minutes by bus from Nara Station.

Nara Dreamland, covering an area of 50 ha. is laid out on a hill named Kurokami. A broad avenue runs through the center of this amusement park, which is divided into four sections—"Adventureland," "Tomorrowland," "Yesterdayland" and "Fancyland." A train running around the park stops at each section.

Gion

Gion is the home of "maiko," teen-aged "geisha" peculiar to Kyoto. The Miyako Odori, or Cherry Dance, is annually performed in April by groups of "maiko" and is one of Kyoto's biggest tourist attractions.

At the Gion Corner set up by the Kyoto Visitors Club in the Yasaka Kaikan Building in Gion-machi, "maiko" dances and other entertainments are staged regularly for the enjoyment of tourists.

Chion-In Temple

Chion-in Temple in Kyoto is one of the largest temples in Japan, founded in the 13th century by Priest Genchi. Most of the present temple buildings were reconstructed in the early 17th century. Among the temple's many structures, the corridor behind the Main Hall is noted for the unique device used in its construction. It is designed to emit a sound somewhat like the song of the "uguisu" (Japanese bush warbler) when someone walks on it. It is the work of Jingoro Hidari, a noted sculptor of the Edo period.

Ryoanji Temple

Ryoanji Temple is one of Kyoto's most noted Zen temples. The temple has a world-famous stone garden consisting of white sand and 15 stones. Flat and oblong-shaped, it is

Stone garden of Ryoanji Temple

covered with white sand and artistically designed with 15 stones. They say the garden has some significance in connection with Zen teachings. Though the whole is decisively simple, it imparts an overwhelming feeling of purity and quiet calm.

Amanohashidate

Amanohashidate (lit. the bridge in heaven) in Miyazu City, Kyoto Prefecture, is one of the famed "Scenic Trio of Japan" along with Miyajima in Hiroshima Prefecture and Matsushima in Miyagi Prefecture. Amanohashidate is noted for its pine-clad sandbar jutting into Miyazu Bay. It is about 3.6 km. long and ranges from 37 to 110 m. wide. The best view of it can be obtained from Kasamatsu Park, which also has a lookout point offering the most scenic view of the entire peninsula. When viewed from between one's legs, Amanohashidate appears as though it were a bridge spanning the heavens.

Izumo Taisha Shrine

The Izumo Taisha Shrine in Taisha-machi, Shimane Prefecture, is one of the most popular Shinto shrines in Japan. It is dedicated to Okuninushi-no-Mikoto, a legendary god, who is said to have founded a state in this district in Japan's pre-historic times. The shrine is among the oldest in the country, with its structures representing an ancient style of Japanese architecture characterized by high floors. The present main building was completed in 1744, and the oratory rebuilt in 1959.

The Izumo Taisha Shrine is particularly noted for its guardian god of marriage. It is said that every October by the lunar calendar the various gods throughout the country leave their own shrines and assemble here to talk about marriage arrangements for the nation's single people. This is why October was once called "Kannazuki" (lit. month without Gods), since not a single god was seen in October in anywhere except Izumo.

Miyajima

Miyajima is a picturesque island situated just off Hiroshima in the Inland Sea, and has long been noted as one of the "Scenic Trio of Japan." With an area of about 30 sq. km. and a circumference of 31 km., Miyajima is well-known for its beautiful Itsukushima Shrine.

The shrine is composed of more than 20 structures connected with one another by corridors, all beautifully painted in vermillion. Since the shrine is built on the beach, the floors of the buildings are about a meter above the level of the beach. When the tide comes in, the shrine looks as if it were floating on the sea. Its orange-colored "torii" gate stands 160 m. out to sea, presenting a striking contrast with the surrounding blue water.

Kintai Bridge

The Kintai Bridge in Iwakuni City, Yamaguchi Prefecture, was built in the 17th century by Hiroyoshi Kikkawa, a feudal lord of the district for the purpose of protecting the area from flooding by the Nishiki River running near his residence. Hence, the bridge is about

Kintai Bridge

12 m. above the water at its highest point. In building the bridge no nails were used. Because of its resemblance in shape to an abacus, the bridge is called "Soroban-bashi," which means "Abacus Bridge."

"Shuhodo"

"Shuhodo," a large stalactite cave, extends beneath the Akiyoshi Plateau, which is situated in the center of western Yamaguchi Prefecture. With a total length of about 10 km., the cave is said to be one of the largest of its kind, not only in Japan but in the rest of the world as well.

Visitors, however, can inspect only that part of it which is provided with facilities for admitting them. This portion is about 1 km. in length, equipped with electric lights and provided with good paths. Visitors can easily explore this part of the cave with the help of a guide in about two hours. "Shuhodo" is open from 8 a.m. to 4:30 p.m. every day.

Naruto Strait

Naruto Strait, which lies between Shikoku and Awaji Island, is noted for its awe-inspiring view of several whirlpools. It is a rather narrow strait, only 1.3 km. wide, and has numerous large and small reefs. A current caused by water flowing from the Inland Sea into the Pacific and vice versa reaches a speed of 20 km. an hour. The water dashes onto rocks in the sea, creating many whirlpools.

Visitors can watch the whirlpools through a telescope set up at a lookout point in Naruto Park in Naruto City, Shikoku. Sightseeing boats are also operated from the boathouse near Naruto Park and visitors can fully enjoy the spectacular view of the whirlpools from the deck of one of those boats. The best time to see the whirlpools is either in the spring or autumn.

Kotohira Shrine

Kotohira Shrine at Kotohira-machi in Kagawa Prefecture is one of the most famous Shinto shrines in Japan. The shrine is built halfway up a 521-m. hill called "Zozu-zan" (lit. elephant's head mountain). The shrine's Main Hall is reached by a long flight of 785 stone steps. The lower portion of the stone-terraced path is lined on both sides with colorful souvenir shops.

The old-fashioned "kago" (litters) are still available to transport the aged or those with weak legs. Visitors can be carried by "kago" halfway up the stone-terraced path, where the "kago" waits for customers returning to the bottom. Visitors can obtain a panoramic view of the Inland Sea from the area of the main shrine building.

Anan Coast

The Anan Coast of Shikoku faces the Pacific Ocean, extending for 200 km. from Anan City in the north to Cape

Muroto in the south. In the northern portion are many fjords and beautiful seascapes, while raging ocean waves break on the southern stretch. Because of its scenic beauty, the Anan Coast is included in the "Muroto-Anan Coast Quasi-National Park."

This part of Shikoku is noted as the place where sea turtles come to lay their eggs.

Uwajima

Uwajima is a port city situated in the southwestern part of Shikoku. It was formerly the castle-town of the Date family, the feudal lord of the province, but is now the area's industrial economic and cultural center. The city is well-known for its Japanese-style bullfighting handed down from the old days. The bullfights take place on July 24 as part of the Summer Festival of the city's Warei Shrine, attracting thousands of spectators from near and far. Uwajima has bullfights several times a year besides those observed in July.

Hirado

Hirado is a historic port on Hirado Island off the western end of Kyushu. As the first port of Japan opened to foreign communication in the middle of the 16th century, Hirado prospered for about a century as the main port for foreign trade until the Tokugawa shogunate moved the base to Nagasaki in 1641. The city retains several relics suggestive of those bygone days—the site of old Dutch and English factories, the old mansion of the Matsuura family, which played an important role in foreign trade in those days. Many Christians still live in Hirado, proving that Christianity has been rooted firmly there since olden times.

Nagasaki

Nagasaki in Kyushu is the old port opening to foreign trade in the 17th century after Hirado Port was closed. It flourished as Japan's sole base for foreign trade after the country was closed to foreign communications. Because of its role as a foreign trade port for such a long period of time, Nagasaki not only contains many historic relics, but also retains a colorful, exotic atmosphere. Its main tourist attractions include the Urakami Catholic Church, Roman Catholic Church, Suwa Shrine connected to German surgeon Philipp Franz van Siebold, Sofukuji Temple with its Chinese-style architecture, the Glover Mansion—said to be the original locale of the opera "Madame Butterfly," the site of the old Dutch firms at Dejima Island and the atom-bomb memorial statue.

Mt. Aso

Mt. Aso (alt. 1,592 m.), rising in the central part of Kyushu, is an active volcano noted for its huge caldera. It consists of five volcanic peaks, of which only one peak is active. The caldera of Mt. Aso is divided into two portions by this group of peaks, each forming a vast plain. The original crater, among the world's largest craters, is 128 km. in circumference and has an area of 255 sq. km. The crater embraces six villages and two local lines of the Japanese National Railways that provide transportation of the area.

"Shiranui"

"Shiranui," or the unidentified fires can be seen on Yatsushiro Bay as well as Ariake Bay in Kyushu. These fires appear on the sea off the beach on the nights of around July 30 and December 31 by the lunar calendar. "Shiranui" is often called "Sendoro" (lit. thousand lanterns) because numerous lights are seen row on row on the sea. They come and go repeatedly. The true sources of these fires had remained unknown until a man named Michika Miyanishi discovered their secret in 1937. Thus, for a long time the fires were called "Shiranui." Mr. Miyanishi explained that the fires were caused by the extraordinary refraction of lights from boats using torches to lure fish at night. The phenomenon occurs when there is any difference between the temperature of the air and the surface of the sea.

Takachiho-Machi

Takachiho-machi in the northern part of Miyazaki Prefecture, Kyushu, is famous for its scenic Takachiho Gorge. Featuring fantastic rock formations, the gorge offers splendid views of nature, including the fresh verdure of spring and the flaming maple leaves of autumn. There are also many places here connected with the birth of ancient Japan. Mythological deities are said to have landed here from the heavens in prehistoric times and ruled over the islands of Japan. Ama-no-iwado (lit. the rock cave of heaven) and Takama-ga-hara (lit. the plain of heaven) here are popular names that also appear in the beginning portions of Japanese mythology.

Miyazaki

Miyazaki, occupying the southeastern part of Kyushu, noted for the Shinto shrine named after it, is sometimes called a city of mythology.

The Pacific coast from Miyazaki down to the Toi Peninsula is full of scenic beauty and abounds in tropical and subtropical plants. The area along this coast has been designated as the Nichinan Coast Quasi-National Park. This part of Kyushu is a popular attraction for young honeymooners.

Cape Toi

Cape Toi at the southwestern extremity of Kyushu is a tableland about 300 m. above sea level. Extending in the Pacific Ocean and embracing Shibushi Bay, Toi is blessed with a mild climate throughout the year. In Misaki Pasture at the tip of the cape some 60 wild horses run free. Valued as a rare species of Japanese horses, they are protected as a "Natural Monument."

Kagoshima

Kagoshima, located on the western shore of Kagoshima Bay, was formerly the castle-town of the Shimazu clan, the "daimyo" (feudal lord) of the district, flourishing for nearly 700 years.

The city has been called the "Naples of the Orient" because of its scenic beauty and mild climate. The city's chief tourist attraction is Sakurajima Island, an active volcano rising in the middle of Kagoshima Bay. Sakurajima has erupted repeatedly in the past, and at the time of the great eruption of 1914, the volcanic isle was finally joined to the Osumi Peninsula by the lava it ejected.

A "Kago" found around Kotohira Shrine

TRADITIONS

"Cha-no-yu," or Tea Ceremony

"Cha-no-yu" is the traditional Japanese art of brewing and serving tea. Sen-no-Rikyu (1521–1591), the great master of the tea cult, succeeded in creating his own unique ceremony based on the art of serving tea. It has survived almost unchanged down to the present day as the fundamental ritual of the tea ceremony. The tea ceremony ranks quite high among the accomplishments expected of young ladies in the same way that flower arranging does, both of which are widely practiced by married as well as unmarried women.

As the first step in preparing the tea, the powdered tea is put in a tea-bowl and hot water boiled in an iron kettle is poured over it. Next, the tea mixture is beaten with a tea whisk until it is thick and frothy like peasoup. Finally, the tea is passed around to the guests, who drink it ceremoniously.

"Ikebana," or the Art of Flower Arrangement

"Ikebana" is the authentic art of flower arranging, in which flowers are arranged according to their own individuality.

The art of flower arrangement has developed side by side with the tea ceremony. In arranging flowers, emphasis is placed on the individual character of the flower and plants, the combination of color and line, the shapeliness of the branches, the leaves of the plants and the kind of vase in which the flowers are arranged. The main place for displaying a flower arrangement is the "tokonoma," an alcove which is found in the best room of a Japanese-style house.

"Bonsai," or Potted Dwarf Tree

"Bonsai" is a potted tree peculiar to Japan. These potted trees are dwarfed and stand only 30 to 50 cm.high. Sometimes the branches of the plants are deliberately twisted or bent in the course of their cultivation to display an artistic variety in their shape. To keep a potted tree alive and to foster its growth, gradually albeit unnaturally, it should be watered a little and placed in the sun at least once a day. Too much water will make it grow more than necessary. The number of leaves on the tree, not to speak of the number of branches, is restricted to the amount of fertilized soil in the pot—just enough to keep it alive. The species of trees used for this purpose include the pine, cypress, maple, oak, plum, cherry and so forth.

Fine Arts and Folk Art

"Ukiyo-e"   "Ukiyo-e" (genre pictures), or Japanese
wood-block prints, are well-known around the world,
especially the excellent prints of Utamaro Kitagawa
(1753–1806), who depicted the beauty of Edo (present
Tokyo) in his works. The "ukiyo-e" made its debut in the
early part of the 17th century. It depicted various scenes
in the lives of Edo residents. Besides Utamaro Kitagawa,
distinguished "ukiyo-e" painters are Hokusai Katsushika
(noted for working out beauty of Mt. Fuji) and Hiroshige
Ando. Especially Hiroshige's "53 stations along the
Tokaido" are well-known landscape works. Their masterpieces, many of which are still preserved, are exceedingly
valued by art connoisseurs.

"Sumi-e"   "Sumi-e," or ink painting, is done with carbon
ink. The subjects selected in "sumi-e" are chiefly natural
scenes, birds and other animals, and flowers and other plants.
Solid delineation is made by adjusting the thickness of ink.
The technique of "sumi-e" painting originated in the 7th
century on the continent and was introduced to Japan at
the beginning of the Kamakura period (1192–1333).

   "Sumi-e" first developed among Zen priest and gradually began to be practiced by professional artists. Sesshu,
a famous "sumi-e" painter of the mid-15th century, was
a Zen priest. "Sumi-e" in those days was adapted to the
decorations on sliding or folding screens, although it was
also retained in the form of hanging scrolls. "Sumi" ink
paintings look simple and static but they are highly prized
because of their artistic value.

Calligraphy   Writing Chinese characters in "sumi" has
been popular and customary with the Japanese for many
centuries. Even today, it is regarded as one of the accom-

plishments of youngsters, and there are many circles that take a keen interest in calligraphy. It is practiced for the purpose of cultivating one's inner self. In calligraphy, particular emphasis is placed on the thickness of the ink, the movement of the writing brush and the combinations of brush strokes in addition to the arrangement of the writing. Thus, the writing is said to manifest the character of the writer as well as the state of mind in which he wrote.

Lacquer Ware As referred to in ordinary English dictionaries as "japan," Japanese-style lacquer coating is well-known to the world.

Most Japanese family soups are served in a bowl made of lacquer ware and sometimes chopsticks are lacquered.

Precious lacquer wares are "maki-e" (polished gold-lacquer), "chinkin" (with the surface decorated in hairline engravings filled with gold leaf) and "choshitsu" (consisting of layers of different-colored lacquer).

Noted lacquer ware products are "Wajuma-nuri" in Wajuma, Ishikawa Prefecture, "Aizu-nuri" in Aizuwaka-matsu, Fukushima Prefecture and "Tsugaru-nuri" in Hiro-saki, Aomori Prefecture.

Chinaware Although specimens of the oldest pottery in Japan are found among the treasures of the 8th century, chinaware (ceramics) was not introduced from China until the 12th century. Since that time, Seto (a city still thriving in Aichi Prefecture) has been one of the main centers of chinaware production and the surrounding area still produces excellent chinaware. Hence, chinaware is often called "seto-mono" (lit. Seto goods).

"Arita-yaki" of Saga Prefecture, "Kyo-yaki" of Kyoto, "Kutani-yaki" of Ishikawa Prefecture, "Satsuma-yaki" of Kagoshima Prefecture and "Mashiko-yaki" of Tochigi Prefecture are other well-known types of chinaware produced in Japan.

Clothing

Kimono   Kimono, the traditional Japanese garment, received considerable development during the Heian period (794–1192). Since that time, the Japanese kimono has undergone various changes, but none of them have been fundamental.

The present kimono, especially that worn by women, is designed with beautiful patterns, mostly flowers and plants, dyed in multicolors. The gorgeous woman's kimono features designs embroidered with gold and silver thread, with the finest kimono being made of silk. Kimonos for middle-aged women have smaller patterns and more subdued backgrounds, while those for men are usually made of plain cloth dyed blue or dark brown.

"Obi"   The "obi," or sash, is one of the essential components of traditional Japanese dress, being used for fixing the kimono on one's body. Women's "obi" are sometimes works of art because of the artistic patterns displayed in the embroidery and gilding. The "obi" is usually tied at the back and serves as a decorative addition to the kimono with its beautiful designs. Heavy brocade, damask silk and other materials are used in today's "obi." The men's "obi" is not decorative, but is dyed in a subdued color, usually dark blue or brown, or black.

"Yukata"   "Yukata," which originally meant a bathrobe, now refers to a kind of unlined kimono made of flax or cotton with printed or dyed patterns and worn in the summertime. Although "yukata" is traditionally considered as a casual home-wear, a recent trend indicates that it is acceptable as Japanese-style summer wear when shopping or even when visiting people. Just before the summer season, "yukata" are displayed for sale at kimono shops or department stores, where even the latest fashions can be seen. Japanese also use "yukata" as a nightgown called "nemaki" all year round, but the same type of "yukata" can never be worn in the daytime once it has been used as a "nemaki."

"Mon"

Every Japanese family has its own crest called "mon" or "kamon." The best-known crest—chrysanthemum with 16 petals—is that of the Imperial Family. Next to the chrysanthemum in popularity among the people is the crest of the Tokugawas, bearing three leaves of the hollyhock. On the official outer garment of the Japanese kimono, the "montsuki" (lit. crest coat), are five crests—one on the back, one on each sleeve and one on each side of the breast. These crests are dyed white on black "montsuki."

"Mizuhiki" and "Noshi"

"Mizuhiki" consists of red-and-white cord (sometimes gold-and-silver cord) properly tied around the gift-wrapping paper of a present to express the sender's appreciation to the receiver. For funeral gifts—monetary offerings to the departed spirit, black or silver and white cord is invariably used instead of red or gold.

"Noshi" is a narrow strip of dried abalone wrapped in a red-and-white paper folder in the shape illustrated here, and pasted on the gift wrapper.

In olden times, "samurai" (warriors) before going

"Mizuhiki" and "noshi"

51

to battle and after returning from successful campaigns, ate abalone since it has a highly-esteemed delicacy and was therefore used to encourage or celebrate "samurai's" endeavors.

"Yukata"-clad woman with "uchiwa"

"Uchiwa," or Fan

"Uchiwa" is a fan made of bamboo and paper. Japanese paper is pasted on a thin bamboo framework that is either circular or shaped like a rough triangle at the end of the handle. The Japanese fan today is mainly used for cooling oneself by fanning and is as much an indicator of the hot season as is the wind bell. It was once included among the main gifts to customers from various stores as part of their summer sales campaign.

In the feudal period, fans were especially designed for warriors. Called "gumbai-uchiwa" (lit. military-control fan), they were used by generals when commanding their army on the battlefield. The "gumbai" now used by referees in traditional sumo (Japanese wrestling) bouts is a replica of the military fan of those days.

"Sensu," or Folding Fan

"Sensu" is a fan that originated in Japan in the Heian period (794–1192) modelled after a fan introduced from China. It folds up when not in use and makes a triangular shape when it is open. Made of bamboo and paper, it was used in olden times by the nobility as a clothing accessory and was often presented as a gift to the nobles from the emperor. Folding fans were used extensively by both men and women in summertime before air-conditioning became so popular. Nowadays, it is commonly used by dancers in performances of the Japanese classical dance. This type of fan is usually lavishly decorated. In fact, some of them are so beautifully and artistically made that they are regarded as a collector's item.

Musical Instruments

"Koto"   "Koto" is a musical instrument unique to Japan, although similar ones can be found in China and Korea. It is a type of harp made from a piece of board less than two meters long and a little over 20 cm. wide. Most "koto" have 13 strings, which are stretched over a bridge on the board. The original "koto" is said to have been introduced from the West through the continent. The "koto" is usually played only on auspicious occasions.

"Shamisen"   "Samisen" or "Shamisen" is a three-stringed musical instrument vaguely resembling a banjo.

It is indispensable with the performance of Japanese music and dancing, and is probably the most popular of all Japanese musical instruments. It was introduced to Japan from China by way of the Ryukyu Islands (now Okinawa Prefecture). The body of the "samisen" is

"Koto" (left) and "shamisen"

composed of three sections—the neck, finger board and the drum-like main section at the end. Both faces of this section are covered with the skin of cats or dogs. The neck and finger board sections together are less than a meter long, and the three strings are graded in thickness to produce ascending tones. To play the "samisen" a large plectrum made of ivory or tortoise shell is used.

"Shakuhachi"   "Shakuhachi," a kind of flute, is made from a bamboo stem and has 5 to 8 finger holes. The tones produced by it are very low and not generally suitable for use in an orchestra, but the flute is good accompaniment to the "samisen" and "koto."

It is about 50 cm. (1.8 "shaku" in the old Japanese unit of measure) long. 1.8 "shaku" is called "isshaku hassun" (for short pronounced "shakuhachi").

"Kagura," or Shinto Dance

"Kagura" is a sacred Shinto dance usually performed at shrine festivals. Its origin is very old, dating back to prehistoric days. It was formerly performed at the Imperial Court as a kind of religious rite in order to console the souls of the dead. The "kagura" today, accompanied by the music of flutes, drums, lutes and gongs, is performed on the festival days of a shrine to invoke divine help or to pray for a bumper crop.

Martial Arts

Karate Karate is one of the arts of self-defense introduced to the Ryukyu Islands (present Okinawa Prefecture) from China in the 16th century. Since no traditional weapons are used in this martial art, it is called "karate," or empty hand. The attack and defense are performed with the fist, elbow, heel, the tip of the toes or the lower knife-edge of the hand called "tegatana" (lit. hand sword). An expert can kill a man with a single stroke of the hand to a vital spot.

Judo Judo is a kind of wrestling based on the centuries-old martial art of "jujutsu" and converted into a modern sport by Dr. Jigoro Kano (1860–1938). Dr. Kano mastered two old "jujutsu" schools and in the 1880's organized modern judo by coordinating the old styles and eliminating their dangerous features.

One's degree in the mastery of judo is identified by the color of belt one wears. For instance, a white belt indicates the lower "kyu" (classes); a reddish-brown belt is for first to third "kyu," a black belt signifies first to fifth "dan" (grade), a red-and-white belt shows sixth to eighth "dan," and a red belt is for ninth or 10th "dan." Today, there are a large number of judo enthusiasts throughout Japan, with various tournaments taking place from time to time, including the All-Japan Championships (with no weight classes) in late April or early May at the Nippon Budokan (Martial Arts Hall) in Tokyo.

Kendo Kendo is the battle-tested Japanese style of fencing, originating from "kenjutsu"—the art of fencing. Kendo flourished in the 13th century Kamakura period.

A kendo match is won by striking one's opponent in one of three parts of his body—"men" (helmet or head), "do" (trunk) and "kote" (forearm)—with a bamboo sword. A referee and three judges decide the winner on the basis of a maximum two-point system.

As in the other traditional martial arts, there are 10 ranks called "dan," with each successively higher rank dependent on the degree of skill and knowledge of the practitioner.

"Aikido" "Aikido" is becoming popular not only in Japan but in many countries around the world because it helps to improve the flexibility of the joints to promote smooth physical movement and can be used to overpower an opponent without risk of injuring him.

The chief difference between "aikido" and judo is that in "aikido" the two contestants remain apart from each other, never giving one another a chance to get a hold, while judo is based on the two contestants holding each other's collar and sleeves. Most "aikido" techniques are based on grasping the opponent's hands and applying pressure or twisting until he submits.

"Naginata" "Naginata," or Japanese-style halberd, was included among the weapons of the 13th century. Rather than being used by the "samurai," however, it was the favorite weapon of the warrior-monks assigned to protect the property of the temples from intruders in feudal days. Low-class "samurai," however, sometimes used them.

In the Edo period (1603–1867), "naginata" became the primary weapon used by women for self-defense.

Today, "naginata" is the chief martial art pursued by women and has often been adopted in school athletic programs for girls.

Japanese Architecture

Wood has long been used as the chief material in the Japanese architecture because of the climatic conditions and natural resources of the country.

Japanese architecture is characteristic of the Japanese sense of good proportion. Fundamentally, architectural structures were not painted. There are some Shinto shrines painted in vermillion, but this is certainly not representative of pure Japanese taste. Although the technique of painting buildings was introduced from China in olden times, generally speaking, Japanese architects valued the natural colors of wood as the basis of their color scheme.

Typical Japanese houses today are built as modifications of the old dwellings that flourished in the 14th to 16th centuries. The present-day Japanese house is a combination of the "buke-yashiki" (lit. warrior's house) and the old houses of the common people, the latter having been very simple like today's country farm houses.

"Tokonoma"

A "tokonoma" is an alcove or square niche built at one end of the best room in a Japanese-style house. A picture or calligraphy scroll is hung on the wall of a "tokonoma," while a vase with arranged flowers, an antique or some other artistic object is placed on the terraced floor.

Since Japanese prefer simplicity to a lot of decoration, the "tokonoma" is the only place used for decorative purposes in a Japanese house. The alcove was used as the family altar in ancient times and is still considered as a place of sanctity. The most honored guest is always seated at dinner with his back to the "tokonoma."

"Kakejiku"

A "kakejiku," or hanging scroll, is used as one of the ornaments in Japanese-style houses. It was imported from China in the 6th century, when Buddhism was introduced to Japan. The subject depicted on ancient scrolls was usually an image of Buddha since they were hung on the wall of a room for the purpose of worship-

"Tokonoma" and "kakejiku"

ping Buddha. However, the subject on the scroll has gradually changed and pictures other than Buddhist figures were painted along with the calligraphy, as can be seen today.

"Byobu"

"Byobu," or folding screen, is a kind of furniture used in a Japanese house. It was commonly used in olden times at temples, shrines, castles, palaces and "samurai" (warriors) mansions. The "byobu" is divided into two or more sections and used as a blind screen or room divider. Thick Japanese paper or cloth, usually silk, covers the wooden frame. Since it can easily be folded up, it is convenient to handle or store. The "byobu" was introduced from China in the 7th century and is commonly decorated with paintings. Gorgeous works of art created on the folding screens were abundantly produced in the 14th to 16th centuries, when an aristocratic culture flourished. It is still a custom in Japan to place a folding screen upside down when someone in the family dies.

"Fusuma"

The "fusuma," or sliding screen, plays an indispensable part in creating separate quarters in a Japanese house. This type of a room divider is probably peculiar to a Japanese-style house, giving it a high degree of flexibility for changing the accommodation capacity of the rooms. Since the sliding screens are easily movable, it is quite easy to make a room either larger or smaller. The sliding screen is made either of wood, or of thick paper or cloth spread on the wooden frame. Pictures of flowers, plants, birds or animals are usually painted on sliding screens.

Excellent works of art were produced on sliding screens in the 16th to 17th century, when several famous Japanese painters appeared one after another. Eitoku Kano, Sanraku Kano, Yusho Kaiho and Tohaku Hasegawa are all well-known artists of that period. Their masterpieces can be seen at the old temples in Kyoto.

"Tatami"

"Tatami" is a thick mat covered with tightly woven rush grass called "igusa." The standard-size "tatami" mat is 1.8 m. long, 0.9 m. wide and 6 cm. thick.

"Tatami" is a natural air-conditioner in absorbing dampness and preventing dryness. The size of a Japanese room is designed on the basis of the number of "tatami" used. For example, a 6-mat room has a square shape (strictly speaking, 3.3 square m.).

Rooms of 4.5 mats, 6 mats, 8 mats and 10 mats are most commonly found in Japanese houses. Even for Western-style rooms without "tatami," the size of room is customarily based on the number of "tatami" that would fit into it.

"Shoji"

A "shoji" is a kind of a sliding door peculiar to the Japanese houses. It is usually made by spreading and pasting Japanese papers on a wooden frame made with the crosspieces overlapping each other. Compared with "fusuma" (sliding screen), the sliding door is generally used to separate the veranda or corridor from the various rooms. "Shoji" are covered with paper or glass to allow the sunlight to penetrate the room.

"Kaya"

"Kaya" (lit. mosquito net) is used to keep away the mosquitos in summertime in a Japanese house. A flaxen net of fine mesh has long been used as the material for making a mosquito net, but these days nylon and other synthetic fibers have come into use along with the traditional flax. Usually oblong in shape, the "kaya" has four or six hangers with which it is hung from the lintels over the bed. The original "kaya" is said to have been imported from the continent in olden times. Some Japanese believe that one can escape lightning by staying under a flax mosquito net.

Castles

Most of the feudal castles in Japan were destroyed during the Meiji period (1868–1912), but there are still some remaining.

A typical specimen of ancient castle is the Himeji Castle in Himeji, Hyogo Prefecture, constructed in 1581. It retains its original form and is noted for its grand and elegant appearance. Osaka Castle in Osaka, first built by Hideyoshi Toyotomi in 1583, is a massive structure and one of the largest castles in Japan. The present building, however, is a reproduction of the original that was completed in 1931.

The Imperial Palace in Tokyo is also an example of a feudal castle, built in 1636 by the Tokugawa Shogun.

Landscape Gardens

Most Japanese landscape gardens are modeled after some natural scene. This is because Japanese take a keen interest in natural beauty and have an unusually sensitive perception of nature. Thus, the art of Japanese gardening is based on the natural arrangement of hills, trees, rocks, waterfalls, streams, and lakes and so forth. Although gardening techniques developed around the appearance of nature, Japanese landscape gardens are not mere copies of nature. Rather, they are reproductions of natural scenery in an elaborate modified form.

"Ishidoro"

"Ishidoro" (lit. stone lanterns) were once associated with Buddhism, since they were used to light precincts of temples in olden times. Some shrines also had stone lanterns. Nowadays, "ishidoro" are used merely for decoration or for lighting Japanese gardens.

"Chochin"

"Chochin" is a Japanese-style lantern made of horizontal bamboo frames covered with paper or silk, collapsible when not in use.

"Chochin" with a candle set in the center of the base plate, was first used for religious rites. Later, it was regarded as the only handy light for nighttime outings.

"Chochins" are now used for decorative purposes at festive evening occasions or hung inside homes during "Bon" season. "Chochin" with rather flashy designs are found at these festive events, while ones with more subdued designs are used in the home.

A typical Japanese landscape garden

SOCIAL LIFE

Rice

Rice, which was rationed for nearly 40 years, can now be purchased without restriction.

To protect rice farmers, the Japanese government buys unpolished natural rice at the rate of ¥17,232 for 60 kg. and sells it to wholesalers at ¥14,771. The difference is borne by the government. Retail rice shops sell polished rice at ¥3,000 for 10 kg. (¥18,000 for 60 kg.), the unit for standard-grade rice. Rice of the highest quality sells from ¥3,700 to ¥4,000 for a 10 kg. unit (the price as of 1977).

The average Japanese eats about 86 kg. of rice a year. Recent trends in eating habits point toward an increase in the use of bread or flour-made foods, causing a decline in rice consumption.

3-C's

The 3-C's stand for car, cooler and color TV as the barometer of modern, civilized life in Japan. Before the mid-1950's, their three predecessors—electric refrigerator, electric washer and electric cleaner—were said to be modern version of the "Three Sacred Treasures of the Imperial Family" (precious jewel, mirror and sword). But the three items were gradually upgraded to accord with rising living standards and now new 3-C's in 1970's are central heating, cabin-cruiser and country home.

Television

The television network has spread so widely to every nook and cranny of Japan that you can enjoy your choice of program no matter where you live in the country—and in color, too, with very few exceptions. In Tokyo, for instance, there are seven different channels (and as many as nine if UHF stations are included), whereas the minimum number of channels is no less than three in smaller cities and towns. Both quasi-governmental and private broadcasting co-exist in Japan, with the former requiring a reception fee.

Money in Circulation

Five kinds of coins are now in circulation—1, 5, 10, 50 and 100 yen. As far as bills currently circulating are concerned, there are four—500, 1,000, 5,000 and 10,000 yen. The once-popular ¥100 bill has completely disappeared.

Faces on Bills

Featured on each of the ¥5,000 and ¥10,000 bills is Prince Shotoku (573–621), who contributed much to the establishment of the imported religion of Buddhism in Japan and who ordered the construction of the Horyuji Temple—

Money in circulation

the world's oldest wooden structure. Hirobumi Ito (1841–1909), whose face appears on the ¥1,000 bill, and Tomomi Iwakura (1825–1883), who is on the ¥500 bill were both politicians in the Meiji era. Ito was Japan's first prime minister in the post-restoration regime.

Deposit System

The deposit business is handled mainly at banks and post offices. Post offices, large or small, are scattered throughout the country and any inter-office handling is freely available. On the other hand, banking business is convenient only within their own branch networks, although the on-line computer system has recently made it possible to widen the scope of transactions with other allied banks. Deposits are limited to ¥3,000,000 at post offices, but there are no limits on bank accounts. However, the government taxes the interest on bank deposits exceeding ¥3,000,000, although tax is exempted on all deposit accounts at post offices. Deposit transactions are handled from 9 a.m. to 3 p.m. at banks and from 9 a.m. to 4 p.m. at post offices.

"Internal Deposit System"

"Internal" in this case means inside companies or corporations. Companies or corporations sometimes serve as private banks for their employees, collecting money from them, and paying less interest to creditors and more interest to depositors in comparison with banks and other financial agencies. Employees may get more benefits and they may spend their money as working funds. Thus, both profit by this "internal deposit system." The only concern on the part of the employees is the fact that employers under some circumstances may pressure them to deposit their bonuses into this system.

Bonuses

In Japan bonuses were originally paid to share some surplus benefits, but today it is customary to pay a bonus regardless of this original background. However, the same principle still remains unchanged—the larger the profits, the larger the bonuses. The average Japanese white-collar worker receives a biannual bonus in June and December equivalent to six times his monthly income. Needless to say, commercialism goes into full swing during the bonus season, with banks and department stores operating a big-scale bonus campaign to "draw water to their own mill."

Public Lotteries

In present-day Japan, the average citizen dreams of acquiring his own house. It is no easy matter to realize this dream, for with a scarcity of suitable land and skyrocketing prices of building materials as well as land, a modest house within the Tokyo city limits can cost him well over ¥10,000,000. However, one get-rich-quick way open to law-abiding citizens is to win in a public lottery. The first prize for lotteries sponsored by local governments was raised to the present 10 million yen in 1968 and there are even lotteries that occasionally offer double this amount for first prize. On the day when the lottery tickets are put on sale, people eagerly line up in long queues in front of the designated banks from early morning hours.

Fortune Tellers

In the dimly lit seclusion of the side streets, branching off from the neon-lit main thoroughfares of such bustling amusement and shopping districts as Shinjuku and Shibuya in Tokyo, you will come upon the stalls of palm-readers. A paper lantern glows atop a rickety table, on which a large magnifying glass and set of divining sticks can be seen. These palmists are mostly older men, with just a few elderly women around. For a modest fee, they examine your palm-lines with the aid of the magnifying glass. Then after asking a few searching questions and consulting the divining sticks which they have arranged on the table with due ceremony, they tell your fortune and give you encouraging advice. At the stalls of the more popular palmists, people wait for their turn to have their palms read. The overwhelming majority of the palmists' customers are young women.

Names of Eras

Since very early in history, it has been the tradition of Japan's Imperial Court to initiate a new era with the accession to the throne of each new emperor, a custom that is said to have been introduced from ancient China. The auspicious names of the eras are chosen by selected scholars after deliberate consulting of old chronicles. The current year, 1979, corresponds to the 54th year of Showa. In addition to the dominical year, the Japanese people are accustomed to using the names of such eras when referring to a specific year.

"Soroban"

The "soroban" originated in China, but was greatly developed in Japan. As shown in the illustration, the Japanese abacus is divided in two sections—upper and lower. It has one row of beads in the upper section, and four rows (or five rows in the old-fashioned type) of

"Soroban"

beads in the lower. Each in the upper section indicates 5, while every bead in the lower section is 1. Each time you move a digit to your left, it is multiplied 10 times. Those skilled in using "soroban" can complete any complicated calculation in just a few moments, and by calling up a mental image of a "soroban," they can even calculate without actually using one. A licensing test is held regularly on a nation-wide scale, and a certificate of full proficiency still carries a lot of weight in one's personal history.

Mini-Computer

This is a time-saving age. Instead of taking time to master how to manipulate a "soroban," more and more people, including young primary and junior high school pupils, now like to use pocket-size electronic computers, a variety of which can be purchased for less than ¥10,000. The mini-computer market is becoming so competitive, in fact, that the price is going down and the computer's capability has been remarkably upgraded to the extent that it can do root calculation in addition to the four basic rules of arithmetic. Nobody denies the convenience of mini-computers, but some people are concerned that they may spoil the basic ability of young school children to calculate.

Cigarettes

The manufacture and sale of cigarettes are monopolized by the Japan Tobacco & Salt Public Corporation. Imported cigarettes are also controlled by the same corporation. Among the most popular domestic brands are Hi-lite, Cherry and Peace. Perhaps in anxiety over the widespread medical warnings, more people prefer filter cigarettes in this country, too. A warning is printed on each package, saying: "Be careful not to smoke too much for the sake of your health."

Tea Rooms and Coffee Houses

Large and small, smartly-styled tea rooms and coffee houses have become indispensable accessories of the busy quarters in the cities and towns of Japan. People come here not just to drink tea or coffee, or to kill time, but also to talk business with a client or to relax with a date. Students also use them as a place to do their homework. Recorded or taped music is continuously played at many of these shops, either as background music or for serious listening. This includes classical music, mood music, jazz, rock or pop, depending on the taste of the clientele. Some teashops specialize in "utagoe," or community singing, where everyone joins in to the accompaniment of guitars.

"Morning Service"

This is a unique Japanese-style service peculiar to coffee

shops. If you go to a coffee shop during the morning hours until, say, 11 a.m., toast or a roll will be served with coffee without any extra charge. In other words, the regular price of coffee covers a combination of coffee, toast or roll and sometimes even a boiled egg. This service is especially popular with students and single office workers.

Bathhouses

Japanese public bathhouses have generally become out-moded in recent years, but this is still a daily necessity for some city dwellers. Common to almost all public bath-houses are a large tiled bathtub and a spacious, tiled floor. Remember: the tub is used only for warming the body, while the floor is for washing it with soap. Be sure to rinse off completely before entering the tub. When women wash their hair, much more hot water is required and thus an extra charge is made for this. In recent years, men's hair has been getting longer so that long-haired men are charged in the same way as women. Most bathhouses are open between 4 p.m. to 11 p.m., and there is no concern about how long it takes to bathe.

Barber Shops

The barber's "set rate" usually covers everything from a shave and a haircut to a shampoo and earpicking as well as a neck and shoulder massage. Manicuring is an exception; Japanese men are generally not interested in having their nails manicured. Almost all barber shops are open on Sundays, but they are closed on Mondays except

Shop signs
Beauty parlor (left) and barber's

in the downtown business districts.

Beauty Parlors

Women, both old and young, now go to a beauty parlor at least once every few months on the average. In Japan, hairdressing is regarded as a rewarding occupation for women, so much so that if your wife happens to be an established hairdresser, as an old saying has it, she can positively afford to support you. One is required to obtain a governmental certificate to work as a hairdresser, as in the case of barbers. Like most of the barber shops, beauty parlors open on Sundays. They close on Tuesdays.

Department Stores

A department store offers everything all under one roof, utilizing every possible idea and every possible hint to attract more customers. A theater, rooftop playground, dining room and a bargain-sale floor are indispensable elements in any department store. In some cases, a huge dining room may take up a whole floor since its best customers are mothers and children on all-day shopping sprees. Most department stores are open between 10 a.m. and 6 p.m., and are closed, as a rule, either on Monday or Wednesday, although a few close on Tuesday or Thursday.

Hospitals

People these days are apt to rush to a hospital, and especially to those large, famous hospitals attached to traditional universities, even if they only suffer from a cold or a stomach-ache. As a result, large hospitals are invariably overcrowded, and it is sometimes necessary to wait for three hours to get a three-minute diagnosis. Dentists are no exception. Some dentists accept patients only on a reservation system, while others flatly say: "No new clients are accepted." Incidentally, there is no system of separating prescription drugs from those freely available on the shelves of a pharmacy or dispensary so that one can purchase almost any kind of drug without a doctor's prescription. There are a few exceptions, of course.

Athletic Clubs

To meet the growing demand for gymnastic exercising, athletic clubs have been increasing by leaps and bounds lately. A recent trend shows that club members mainly consist of weight-watchers, both men and women. Accordingly, exercises designed to work off their excess poundage are the most popular.

The membership fee varies from ¥3,000 to ¥200,000 a year, depending on the gym facilities available. In addition to the membership fee, an extra charge is usually required for each type of exercise facility one uses.

Telephone

The national popularization rate of telephones now exceeds 57%, and the automatic dialing system is making rapid progress. At present time, the telephone charge is comparatively cheap—10 yen for local calls, or approximately $\frac{1}{3}$ that of the United States and $\frac{1}{4}$ that of West Germany.

"Push-Phones"

True, this is a new-type of telephone, but its usage is much more practical than it might seem at first and it is much more versatile than a regular dial phone. It is almost like a small home computer capable of calculating, reserving Shinkansen superexpress tickets and memorizing the most frequently used telephone numbers. Its future possibilities are boundless. However, the basic charge is quite a bit more expensive than the regular type.

Electricity

Electric voltage is 100V a.c. throughout Japan, (at hotels

as well as private homes). Foreign tourists should, there-fore, be careful not to use their 220V electric razors and other appliances of the same voltage. As far as electric frequency is concerned, there are two different cycle sys-tem—50 Hz in the eastern half, including Tokyo, 60 Hz in the western half, including Osaka and Kyoto. This makes it necessary even for the Japanese to use a fre-quency convertor for their electric appliances when they move from one cycle area to another.

Water Supply

Japan used to be proud of its pure, good-quality water. In recent years, however, the centralization of population in big cities has made it difficult to keep a supply of water that meets the need for quantity as well as quality, although in terms of quality one can still drink as it is. In some local areas, water of good, natural taste is still abundant, and it is this water that makes the taste of Japanese "sake." Naturally, the consumption of water rises considerably during the dry, hot summer months. As a result, the supply of water runs short, causing a suspension or a decrease in the use of water so that it may be supplied only during certain hours.

Toilets

If you want to wash your hands or relieve yourself when you are away from your home or office, you can use the toilets at almost all railway stations, national or private. Another idea is to walk into a department store, hotel or office building, where a toilet is usually located on every floor. The latter are cleaner than public toilets at stations, which are open to practically any passer-by. Restaurants and coffee shops may offer timely help, too.

Sexual Expressions

The government regulates sexual expression with certain limits in writing, painting and photography. Too much bodily exposure is blotted out and violators are punished under the Minor Offenses Act. Although pornography is permitted in some foreign countries, it is against the law in Japan to sell or possess any imported pornography.

Newspapers report that some of the late-night TV programs contain many sexually provocative scenes that almost go beyond the limit of the law.

Legal Holidays

There are 12 legal holidays a year on the current Japanese calendar. If one falls on Sunday, you can expect a long weekend since it is celebrated on the following Monday. Between the end of April and the early part of May, Japan has a holiday-studded season commonly called "golden week." Since this is also the ideal tourist season, millions of holiday-makers travel extensively at home and abroad.

Roof-Top "Beer Gardens"

Reflecting the present beer-drinking boom, roof-top "beer gardens" in the metropolitan areas do a flourishing business during the summer time. These beer gardens, set up on the roofs of tall office buildings, command a fine view of the neon-lit city sprawling below. They also provide welcome relief from the heat of summer evenings, most of them opening around 5 p.m. and closing between 9 and 10 p.m. Draught beer is naturally the most popular item on the menu, but bottled beer, soft drinks and light snacks are also served. At some places, band music and floor shows are even provided.

"Hokosha tengoku" at Ginza Street

"Hokosha Tengoku," or Pedestrian Paradise

Traffic congestion in Tokyo reached such an alarming stage that in June 1973 the Metropolitan Police Department decided to ban vehicular traffic from some of its main thoroughfares on Sundays and national holidays, following the example of New York City in providing its citizens with more space and a chance to stroll freely through the very heart of the capital city. The longest of these "pedestrian paradises," and probably the longest of its kind in the world, is the 5.5-km. section that stretches from Ueno to the southern end of the Ginza via Akihabara and Nihombashi.

Red Lanterns

Paper lanterns still have many uses in present-day Japan,

including the indispensable part they play at festivals. Huge lanterns adorn the entrances to many shrines and temples, while in private homes lanterns hung from the eaves add a feeling of coolness to gardens in summertime. The so-called "aka-chochin," or red lantern, has still another popular use—to show the location of cozy drinking houses and small restaurants off the main streets where good "sake" and good food are offered at very reasonable prices. Many office workers in the cities have their own favorite "aka-chochin" shops. After work, they visit these places in small groups and spend an hour or two hobnobbing with their colleagues before starting for their homes.

New-Type Station Buildings

In Japan, a railway station, particularly one located along the Japanese National Railways, very often forms the heart of the surrounding area, and there is a new tendency to build high-rise station buildings under the joint project of national or private railway companies plus local private investors. The lower floors, of course, serve as the railway terminal, while the upper floors are devoted to stores, restaurants and, in some cases, even a hotel. This type of building is called in Japanese "minshueki," or literally a station built partly with private funds.

"Kisei" or Heading Home on Vacation

Quite a large number of Japan's urban dwellers originally came from the country. Twice a year, there is a largescale exodus from Tokyo. One of these occasions is the "Bon Matsuri" (festival of lanterns) in mid-August when people visit the graves of their ancestors and families gather to attend the Buddhist rites. The other exodus takes place at the year-end when people hurry home to celebrate the New

Year with their relatives according to traditional customs. On these occasions, all trains leaving Tokyo as well as other means of transportation are packed full with homeward bound passengers. To reserve seats on the trains, people form long lines at railway stations and in front of travel agencies on the morning tickets go on sale.

Pets

The most popular pets in Japan are dogs, followed by cats, birds, goldfish and, in some cases, even monkeys and turtles. More often than not, dogs are kept outdoors, and owners are obliged to keep their dogs on a leash. It is against the law to let your dogs run free.

Red Feather Campaign

The Red Feather (Akai Hane) campaign originated in 1913 in Cleveland, Ohio, U.S.A., and has been a part of social welfare activities in Japan since 1948. Donations made to the Red Feather campaign are used for such welfare facilities as medical institutions, homes for the aged and homes for the feebleminded.

Cub scouts calling out to passers-by to buy Red Feathers crowd the railway stations and busy sections of the city during the first few days of the campaign. The campaign usually extends from October 1 to December 31 of the year.

There are expectations that donations will reach 7,500 million yen in 1977.

Radio Broadcasting in English

The U.S. military-operated Far East Network (FEN) broadcasts radio programs that can be heard throughout most of the country. The programs consist of news, music, drama, sports, including live sumo coverage, and Sunday chapel service. It is interesting enough to attract many

Japanese listeners, especially the younger generation, as good media for learning English as well as for providing up-to-date information on American hit songs.

English-Language Newspapers

The Asahi, Mainichi and Yomiuri, Japan's three major vernacular newspapers, issue their own English dailies—the Asahi Evening News, Mainichi Daily News and Daily Yomiuri, respectively. The Japan Times does not print a Japanese-language edition, but enjoys the largest circulation among foreigners.

Sunday Carpenters

This is connected with the economic inflationary tendency in Japan. When a Japanese house needs minor repairs, it costs from ¥8,000 to ¥10,000 per day to hire a professional carpenter. As a result, "do-it-yourself" carpenters are increasing in number in an attempt by house owners to save the money that would otherwise be paid to the professional carpenter. The Japan Sunday Carpenters Club has recently been organized with some 40,000 members. Mr. Kikuo Matsushita, chairman of the club, is kept busy appearing on TV programs demonstrating how to become a Sunday carpenter.

"Demae" or Noodle Delivery Man

The acrobatic noodle delivery man, who invariably amused and amazed visitors from abroad, have all but disappeared from the city streets due to the increasingly heavy automobile traffic in recent years. Japanese are avid noodle eaters, and many office workers in the urban areas order noodles for their lunch. When the noodle orders are ready at the noodle shop, the delivery man sets out for the office building of the customer. He bicycles through the streets, balancing a large tray on which are stacked many bowls and box-like containers of noodles. Some of the most skilled delivery men of a few decades ago are said to have carried stacks more than 1-m. high weighing 5 kg. Motorbike equipped with special devices for carrying bowls of noodles without spilling the soup are rapidly replacing the bicycles of the delivery men.

Noodle delivery man

MANNERS AND CUSTOMS

Marriage

Wedding   The average age of newlyweds is 26.8 years for men and 24.5 years for women, according to a survey conducted in Tokyo in 1975. Partly because of Japan's rapid economic growth over the past few decades and the resultant increase in income, especially of the younger generation, people are marrying at a younger age than ever before. On the other hand, so that young couples can cope with soaring house rents, both husband and wife are increasingly obliged to work after their marriage. According to a government report in 1975, the divorce rate in Japan stood at 1.07 per 1,000 population as against 4.60 in the United States and 3.00 in the Soviet Union.

Marriage by Interview   The Japanese name for it is "miai-kekkon." "Miai," or the first meeting of an eligible young man and a marriageable young woman, is arranged by a go-between, who is usually an elderly man or woman of good social standing, and, more often than not, a friend or relative of one of the two families involved. At the "miai," the young man and the woman are usually accompanied by their parents. After this first interview, it is the usual custom for the couple to date several times before making the final decision. Statistics show that "miai" marriages account for as high a proportion as 37.2% of all marriages.

Betrothal Gifts   Once an engagement is announced, the bridegroom is expected to send gifts or money to the bride, the value or amount depending on the locality. It was once the custom to send specific gifts of good omen such as sea tangle, dried cuttlefish and bonito, but cash seems to be the thing to send these days. Some people still follow the practice of "yuino-gaeshi," or returning 50% of the betrothal money to the groom. If the marriage does not materialize after betrothal gifts have been sent, they must be returned. On the other hand, the bride may keep the gifts or money even in the case of divorce just after the marriage.

Bridal School   These finishing schools continue to flourish in Japan. Some bridal schools in the large cities have enrollments running into the thousands. The curricular at these finishing schools vary from one institution to the other, but usually include courses in cooking, dressmaking (both Western dress and kimono), nursing, makeup and hair styling as well as training in such traditional Japanese arts as "cha-no-yu" (tea ceremony), "ikebana" (flower arranging) and calligraphy. Training in playing traditional musical instruments is also offered at some of the schools. It is reported that among the bridal-school students, those having a university degree or a junior college diploma have been increasing in number over the past few years.

Workdays in a Week

The five-day workweek was first adopted by a Japanese company in 1973, but it is now observed by almost 44 percent of all business and industrial firms. To cope with this "shukyu futsuka sei" (lit. two days off a week), some companies have slightly modified it by giving a day off on alternative Saturdays or by extending their working hours on the other days to offset the time lost by the extra day off. Recently, an electric appliance firm created a stir in the business world by adopting a four-day workweek and reports that so far it has been a success.

Sauna Baths

Saunas have taken root in Japan's large cities. Many of them are equipped with hot-water baths of three different temperatures in addition to the regular sauna room. Masseurs are often available, and TV sets are standard equipment in many sauna rooms. In some cases, saunas form part of a larger leisure center along with bowling lanes and other recreational facilities. A number of city hotels have installed saunas of their own for the benefit of their guests.

Turkish Baths

So far as bathing facilities are concerned, there is not much difference between sauna baths and Turkish baths. Perhaps the only real difference is that every Turkish bathhouse has girl attendants to massage the customers after they have had a bath. But now even sauna baths are offering female masseuses. From time to time, there are outcries in the Diet and elsewhere over the embarrassing social problems created by Turkish baths.

"Furoshiki"

It is said that "furoshiki" was originally a cloth spread on the floor to wipe one's feet after taking a bath. Another version tells us that it was once used to wrap up one's clothes in a public communal bath. "Furo" means bath and "shiki" is a cloth to be spread. "Furoshiki," a scarf-like cloth, is used for wrapping and carrying things these days, although it is gradually being replaced by shopping bags, hand bags, shoulder bags and brief cases.

Twelve Signs of the Zodiac

The 12 signs of the Oriental zodiacal cycle, assigned to successive years, in their proper order are: "ne" (rat), "ushi" (ox), "tora" (tiger), "u" (hare), "tatsu" (dragon), "mi" (serpent), "uma" (horse), "hitsuji" (sheep), "saru" (monkey), "tori" (cock), "inu" (dog) and "i" (wild boar). These signs originated in ancient China. According to one popular legend, these 12 animals once held a race, which the wild boar won with the dog finishing second and the rat coming in last. The finishing order in the race was reversed when the animals were allotted to a cycle of 12 years. The zodiacal signs have also been used for denoting compass directions as well as the hours of the day.

Unlucky Numbers

The Japanese regard 4 and 9 as unlucky numbers, for the words "shi" (4) and "ku" (9) are the respective homonyms of the words meaning "death" and "suffering" or "pain." (Curiously enough, if you add 4 and 9, you get 13—an unlucky number in the West.) No hospital rooms or wards are numbered 4 and 9; even in pinball parlors you will look in vain for machines with these unlucky numbers. When a large group of tourists go on a sightseeing tour in a fleet of chartered buses, you will note that there is no Bus No. 4. The bus which immediately follows Bus No. 3 is No. 5.

Lucky Day, Unlucky Day

Most of the wedding ceremonies in Japan are held on "Taian" days, while "Butsumetsu" days are almost always avoided. "Taian", "Butsumetsu" and "Tomobiki" are three of a recurring sequence of six days known as "Rokuyo." When fixing dates for important events and undertakings, "Taian" is the lucky, "All is well" day, while "Butsumetsu" is the unlucky day because of its association with Buddha's death. "Tomobiki" was originally a day "for better or worse," but later came to be interpreted as "dragging in (biki) friend (tomo)." For this reason, "Tomobiki" days are shunned for holding funerals, with some crematories even closing on these days.

Superstitions

As is the case in most countries around the world, Japan also has its share of superstitions that are traditionally believed by the general public. To name a few: when a photograph is taken of three people, the person in the middle will meet bad fortune or even death in the not-too-distant future. "Sanrimbo," an unlucky day on the lunar calendar means to burn down three adjacent houses. People avoid starting the construction of their houses on that day for fear that their neighbors will oppose it and that once it is built, their house will surely burn down. Generally, there are two "Sanrimbo" days in every month.

"Meishi"

If you plan to do business in Japan or with the Japanese,

the first thing you should do is to have your "meishi," or business cards, made up. "How do you do?" greetings and the exchange of business cards are almost inseparable actions in the Japanese way of conducting business introductions. Otherwise, you will probably be asked: "May I have your card?" With this as a background, the Japan Air Lines (JAL) once made 100 or so "meishi" for each of its business-bound passengers flying to Japan. Foreigners like to have their names printed on both sides of their "meishi"—in their own language on one side and in the corresponding Japanese on the other. Quick-working printers can make your "meishi" while you wait.

"Chindon-ya"

This is a small rinky-dink band hired to publicize the opening of a new store or some special sale. It usually consists of three or four musicians dressed in colorful, traditional costumes. The band plays in front of the sponsor's shop for a while and then starts parading the streets in the neighborhood. In many cases, a man beats a big bass drum and cymbals strapped in front of him, while his wife accompanies him to hand out sales flyers. The band also includes a couple more members playing a saxophone, clarinet and/or a trumpet.

Flower Wreaths

Huge floral wreaths enclosed within red-and-white striped frames are often found at the entrance of newly-opened or redesigned shops, stores and restaurants sent by their sponsors, coordinators or friends. Usually, the sender's name is written in large characters to celebrate the opening. "Pachinko" parlors leave these big wreaths outside longer than usual to invite customers' attention.

Black-and-white framed wreaths are sent for funerals

Flower wreaths

or on the night of the wake for the deceased.

"Noren" Curtains

The short curtains hanging in the doorways of many shops in Japan are called "noren." They are hung at the entrance of shops, Japanese-style restaurants, public houses, pawn shops, etc. The designs or characters decorating these "noren" usually indicate the nature of the shop's business and sometimes the "noren" is of great hereditary value. Today, artistic "noren," similar to the authentic shop curtains, are often used to decorate the sitting room or kitchen in private homes.

"Daruma"

"Daruma" is the Japanese equivalent of Bodhidarma, the Indian Buddhist saint of the 6th century, who is believed to have sat for nine long years in meditation to found the Zen sect of Buddhism. The name is usually given to those red papier-mache dolls, representing the saint in

87

meditation and weighted at the bottoms so that they always bob up again whenever they are knocked over. Merchants and even politicians in hopes of success often use "daruma" as a sort of goodluck mascot, since it suggests a spirit that will not be defeated but will keep bobbing up again despite repeated failures. They customarily buy one-eyed "daruma" and paint in the blind eye when success has been achieved.

"Maneki-neko"

"Daruma"

"Maneki-Neko" or Beckoning Cat

As you enter the premises of a Japanese-style restaurant, you will probably notice the figure of a large, grinning cat with one paw raised, sitting on a shelf that faces the entrance. A small, specially made cushion is sometimes provided for it to sit on. This is "maneki-neko," or the beckoning cat, supposed to have the power to bring good business and wealth to the restaurant proprietor. Beckoning cats are made of either papier-mache or porcelain, and their bodies are painted in bright colors. In Japan, as in many countries of the world, cats are believed to be possessed of occult powers, be they good or bad. In the case of the "maneki-neko," the cat is regarded as a good, friendly provider.

"Tachi-Shoben"

"Tachi-shoben" flatly means to urinate outdoors along the road or in the street. To imagine that this is a common daily practice in present-day Japan is like imagining that kimono-clad geisha leisurely stroll through the streets everyday, but it is true that this distasteful male habit has not yet been eliminated. In doing "tachi-shoben," Japanese men seem to prefer finding a target first; e.g., the root of a tree, a wall or a telephone pole. Some Japanese insist it is a national disgrace and most foreigners frown at such scenes, but still for some Japanese men "tachi-shoben" gives them a chance to refresh themselves in free and open air of nature.

"Hachimaki"

If you go to a Shinto festival and watch the procession of shrine palanquins (or portable shrines), you will probably notice that the bearers of the heavy palanquins wear a kind of twisted cloth around their heads. Such a headband is called a "hachimaki." The piece of cloth is simply a cotton hand-towel, dyed in a pattern that indicates the group or area to which the palanquin bearer belongs. A "hachimaki" is supposed to give the wearer special vigor and an increased ability to concentrate. Certainly it serves the added practical purpose of preventing perspiration from running into one's eyes. The expression "wearing a twisted hachimaki (neji-hachimaki or nejiri-hachimaki)" means doing something with all one's might. "Neji-hachimaki" are sometimes worn by students studying hard for important examinations, and by athletes such as marathon runners as well as by workers engaged in manual labor.

Flu Masks

Foreign visitors coming to Japan for the first time and happening to arrive during the winter months are often surprised to see quite a number of Japanese on the streets, in the shops as well as on the trains and subways wearing white gauze masks similar to those worn by doctors and nurses in hospitals. These are "flu masks," worn both by people cautiously trying to protect themselves from catching a cold and those who already have a cold but are being careful not to spread germs or unpleasantness to others by their sneezing and coughing.

"Semba-Zuru"

"Semba-zuru" is a string of a thousand small, folded-paper crane. "Origami," or the art of paper-folding, has always been a popular pastime with the children of Japan and their mothers. With a little practice, almost anyone can fold a piece of paper into the shape of a boat, bird, helmet, flower and so on. Because of its simple elegance, the crane is generally acknowledged to be the masterpiece of the paper-folding art. "Semba-zuru" is often used as a gift to console and encourage someone who is in sorrow or suffering since it conveys the sincerity and good wishes of the sender, who has probably devoted several days painstakingly folding a thousand small cranes.

"Chugen" and "Seibo"

"Chugen" was originally a formal occasion set aside to worship ancestors on July 15 of the lunar calendar, but it has been drastically commercialized in the present-day calendar. The modern "chugen" season now ranges from the beginning to the middle of July, when presents are sent to one's relatives, patrons, business customers and office seniors (never vice versa). Department stores, the ideal places for selecting "chugen" presents, each hold their own special "chugen" sale at this time of the year, constituting one of their major and most competitive annual events.

"Seibo" is the year-end version of the current "chugen" custom. Presents are apt to be more expensive at the year-end season, however.

Summer Greeting Cards

It is customary to send friends and relatives a "how are you getting along?" card during the hottest days of summer in the latter part of July. Every year the government issues a couple of specially designed post cards to suit the occasion. A variety of commercial greeting cards featuring cool colored bamboo leaves, a stream, etc. are also sold at this time of the year.

New Year's Cards

The Japanese custom of sending New Year's cards is quite similar to the Western practice of exchanging Christmas cards, which is generally used on this special occasion as a greeting to relatives, friends of all kinds, classmates and teachers. People send this "nenga hagaki" card even to their very old friends whose faces are long forgotten. Sometimes one receives one of these cards from some unexpected person, who is most probably planning to run for the next election. The total number of cards annually issued by the Ministry of Post and Telecommunications amounts to approximately 2,800 million—about 26 times as many as the total Japanese population. These "nenga hagaki" have proved to be a gold mine for the above-mentioned governmental ministry.

"Hatsuyume"

"Hatsuyume" (lit. the first dream of the year) is a dream that one had on the night of January 2. The dreams are usually ranked according to their quality. The best one is Mt. Fuji, regardless of whether it is seen clearly or is partly obscured by clouds. Next comes a hawk followed by an eggplant. There is no ranking for other types of dreams. The type of dream each member of the family had the previous night is discussed on the morning of January 3.

"Amida-Kuji"

"Amida-kuji" ("kuji" means drawing lots), often short-ened to just "amida," is a friendly way of clubbing money to buy refreshments at afternoon tea time in offices, at home among brothers and sisters, and in school dormi-tories. The word "amida" is derived from Amitabha—the name of the most reversed of the Buddhist deities. The association of the sacred name with this popular game originated in the fact that the lines drawn on a piece of paper for the participants to make their draw, in the shape of the sticks of a folding fan, resembled the rays of Amitabha's halo as represented in Buddhist picture scrolls.

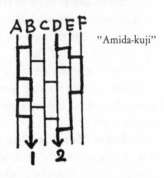

"Amida-kuji"

"Jan-ken-pon"

The Japanese equivalent of tossing up or flipping a coin is a little game called "janken." This is simpler and quicker than a toss up since it required only the hand. Each participant in this game holds out a hand to repre-sent any one of the following three things—a stone, a piece of paper and a pair of scissors. At the same moment, he shouts "jan-ken-pon," equivalent to the English "one, two, three." The closed hand represents a stone, the open hand is paper and two extended fingers the scissors. The idea is that the stone can be wrapped in the paper, but cannot be cut by the scissors, which in its turn can cut the paper. In other words, paper beats stone, stone beats scissors and scissors beats paper.

"Jan-ken-pon"

"Jintan"

Although "Jintan" is one of the brand names of pill-sized deodorants designed to prevent bad breath, it is generally understood by the Japanese to take in the entire range of this kind of oral deodorant just as "Lavoris" is regarded as a catch-all name for anti-germ mouth sprays in the United States.

"Jintan" pills as small as buckshot are sold in a small container with a hole for dispensing them at the top. Many smokers carry "Jintan."

"Shobu" Bath

The flower associated with the Boys' Festival on May 5 is the Japanese iris, partly because this attractive flower begins to bloom about this time of the year and partly because of a play on words. "Shobu," the Japanese name for iris, is homonymous with the word meaning "martial valor." One of the age-old customs observed on the day of the Boys' Festival is to take a "shobu" bath. Iris leaves are dipped in the bath tub, imparting to the bath water a refreshing fragrance as well as a medical value.

"Kotatsu"

This is a typical Japanese-style heating device used during

winter. Originally, charcoal or briquette served as an ideal heating fuel. In those days, a fire was made with charcoal or briquette and then put in a huge clay pot half full of ashes. A wood turret was necessary so that the heat could be held in by a quilt. This heating device was either on the "tatami"-mat floor or in a large square hole in the floor about 30 cm. deep. The temperature of the fire could be adjusted by controlling the ashes. In recent years, however, electricity has taken its place and the electric "kotatsu" is now popular for its cleanliness and convenience. An infrared system is a big seller.

"Hibachi"

"Hibachi" is a Japanese brazier for warming your hands, while the "kotatsu" is mainly devised to warm your feet. Kindled pieces of charcoal are put in a large pot made of chinaware, metal or wood and half-filled with ashes. Particularly in rural areas, people used to warm their feet in the "kotatsu" in winter and bake Japanese rice cakes over this "hibachi." Since neither served as a heater capable of warming the whole room the air in the room always remained cold. In recent years, a variety of modern heaters using oil, gas or electric and capable of warming the entire living space are replacing the old heating devices. And some private homes are now being equipped with a central heating system so that "hibachi" are gradually disappearing.

English Words "Made in Japan"

Today, there are many Japanese words which owe their origin to foreign languages. Most of these come from English language, but are adopted with a pronunciation and meaning that are more or less Japanese. In addition to these, there are quite a number of words and abbreviations in daily use among the Japanese which many people believe to be of English origin, but which are actually pseudo-English. There are instances of some Japanese contrived English words finding their way back into English.

Below are a few of the Japanese-made English words and abbreviations:

after-service . . . . after sales service
back mirror . . . . rear-view mirror
departo . . . . department store
DK (dining room and kitchen) . . . . dinette
lemon tea . . . . tea with lemon
model change . . . . changing models
nighter . . . . night game
romance seat . . . . deluxe reclining seat

Geisha

Geisha, literally meaning an art person, is a product of the Edo period (1603–1867). Geisha are costumed in elaborate kimono and "obi" plus "tabi" (Japanese-style sock, the tip of which is split in two parts). Geisha usually have their glossy, jet-black hair made up in a beautiful coiffure (some geisha wear wigs).

Geisha is understood in Japan to mean an entertainer serving her customers by dancing and singing to the accompaniment of musical instruments such as "samisen" (three-string Japanese banjo) and drum. A geisha attends her customers singly or in groups. When group visits are made to hot-springs and similar resort areas, local geisha girls usually entertain the group.

"Shayo-Zoku"

The night clubs and bars in Tokyo's Ginza are said to be the most expensive anywhere in the world, but they were doing a roaring business until the recent "oil shock" somewhat reversed the tide. This is explained by the fact that practically all the patrons have been "shayo-zoku"—a collective name given to corporation executives, section chiefs and clerks who spend heavily on their firm's expense account. Only these "expense-account plutocrats" could afford the exorbitant prices charged at the high-class restaurants and fashionable night spots.

Office Outings

It is customary for Japanese business firms to organize short overnight trips for their employees once or twice a year by way of rewarding them for their services and also to create a better rapport among the members of the staff. Every member of the company, from the president down to the youngest clerk, joins the outing. The popular destinations are hot-spring resorts within two or three hours' train ride from the city. On arriving at the resort and after soaking in a refreshing hot-springs bath, everyone gathers in a large, "tatami"-floored banquet hall of the "ryokan" for the dinner party. During dinner and the drinking exchange of "sake" cups, the more talented members vie with each other in entertaining the others with songs, comic dances, conjuring tricks or improvised theatricals.

"Bonen-Kai" or Forgetting the Old Year Party

Year-end parties in Japan are commonly called "bonen-kai," or parties for "forgetting the year." This means consigning to oblivion the unpleasant memories and unhappy incidents connected with the passing year and preparing oneself to welcome the New Year in a serene, unblemished frame of mind. These year-end gatherings are mostly drinking parties. People with a wide circle of acquaintances and friends have a busy time during December arranging and attending the "bonen-kai" of office colleagues and business acquaintances.

A dinner party seen in an office outing

ANNUAL EVENTS

New Year

New Year's Day   New Year's Day is the most joyous, and, at the same time, the most solemn occasion for the entire nation. There are many time-honored customs related to this holiday season. The decoration on either side of the entrance to a house is called "kadomatsu," or gate pine. It consists of branches of pine, plum and bamboo, all denoting longevity. At the entrance is a festive rope called "shimekazari," which is decorated with a "daidai" orange and fern leaves. The word "daidai" means "from generation to generation," while fern leaves suggest expanding prosperity. On the morning of New Year's Day, the family members gather in the parlor and exchange greetings. Then they drink sweetened and spiced "sake" called "toso," and enjoy a repast of "zoni"—rice cakes cooked in elaborately prepared soup, and a variety of special New Year's dishes.

"Hatsumode" Early in the morning on New Year's Day, the Japanese people customarily pay their first visit of the year to their tutelar shrines or to well-known Buddhist temples to pray for happiness and good health for themselves and their families for the coming year. This visit is called "hatsumode." Some people leave home well before midnight, and while the temple bells are still ringing out the old year, early arrivals begin to crowd the precincts of the shrines and temples. Good luck talismen or arrows are sold at stalls set up in the precincts. Meiji Shrine is the most popular "hatsumode" shrine in Tokyo.

"Kakizome" "Kakizome" (lit. first handwriting of the year) is perfomed on January 2. The calligraphic writing is done with a Japanese brush and "sumi" (carbon ink) on a slender rectangular piece of white paper to be hung as a scroll immediately after the calligraphy is finished. Most primary and middle schools stage "kakizome" contests at the school's public hall and prizes are given for the best calligraphy.

The theme for "kakizome" contests are usually related to some New Year's event or sometimes a slogan endorsing a New Year's resolution.

Battledore and Shuttlecock The favorite outdoor game of Japanese girls during the New Year holiday season is "battledore and shuttlecock." In this rather simple game, the players hit a shuttlecock back and forth with their battledores as if playing badminton but without a net between them. As a spectacle, however, it is very colorful

because many of the girls are dressed in beautifully patterned, long-sleeved kimono, and not a few of them have
their hair done up in the elaborate, traditional coiffure.
Their battledores, too, are heavily decorated. Sometimes,
when the participants are close friends or family members,
they adopt playing rules by which the loser in each game
has her face smeared with carbon ink or rouge.

Kite-flying Kite-flying has long been the favorite game
of Japanese boys at New Year's. Large-scale kite-flying
contests and kite fights are held in many parts of the
country. The best known of these events is the Kite Fights
at Hamamatsu in Shizuoka Prefecture (early May). Kites
flown measure up to 8 m. long and 7 m. wide, and
require closely coordinated teamwork by hardy men. Kites
with specially treated strings are maneuvered so that one's
own strings cut the opponents' kite strings.

New Year's Parade of Firemen

On the sixth day of January every year, the Tokyo fire
brigades hold their New Year's parade. Acrobatic stunts at
the top of long bamboo ladders, performed by firemen as
part of the parade, thrill the spectators and attract thousands
of people from far and wide. Firemen from all sides brace
the ladders with hooked "tobiguchi" poles. This performance purports to show the agility of the fire-fighters of
old Edo (present Tokyo) when they were confronted
with danger.

Bean-Throwing Ceremony

"Setsubun" or the last day of winter according to the lunar
calendar, falls on Feb. 3 or 4. On the night of "Setsubun,"
people scatter parched beans inside and outside their houses,
shouting "Devils out, Fortune in!" to purify the house
against potential evil. It is a time-honored Buddhist ritual.

Bean-throwing ceremony

There is also a popular belief that if you eat as many of
these beans as the number of years in your age, you will
be assured of good health during the ensuing year.
Large-scale "bean throwings" take place at many of the
Shinto shrines and Buddhist temples.

"Hina Matsuri"

The doll festival, known in Japan as "Hina Matsuri," is
a special festival for girls. So called because it features a
group of dolls on display, this pretty fete is annually celebrated on March 3. A set of "hina" dolls and miniature
household articles are carefully arranged on small, specially
made shelves covered with red cloth. A set of dolls usually
includes an emperor and empress, their ministers, court
ladies, musicians and footmen—all clad in ancient period
costumes. This festival is also called "Momo-no-Sekku," or
peach festival, because peach-blossom twigs often add to
the beauty of the colorful stand of dolls.

"Higan" Weeks

The spring and autumn equinoctial weeks are known as "Higan" periods. All Buddhist temples throughout the country hold special services during these two weeks and people visit the graves of their ancestors to pray for the souls of the departed. "Higan" weeks also signify the changing of the seasons. As one saying puts it: "No heat or cold lasts beyond the equinox."

"Tango-no-Sekku"

Just as the girls of Japan have their own festival on the third day of the third month, the boys celebrate theirs on the fifth of the fifth month. This is called "Tango-no-Sekku" or boys' festival. On this day, miniature suits of armour and dolls representing warriors and legendary heroes are displayed in the house and huge cloth or paper carp called "koinobori" are flown from tall poles over the rooftop. Since the carp is regarded as a courageous fish because it swims upstream past waterfalls and many other obstacles, boys should follow its example by growing up strong and healthy, and rising to greatness by overcoming all difficulties.

"Tanabata"

Star Festival ("Hoshi Matsuri"), also called "Tanabata," is a colorful festival annually celebrated on July 7, although it is held in some localities a month later. On this occasion, people set up bamboo branches in their gardens and tie colorful strips of paper bearing poems on them as an offering to the heavenly lovers—the Weaver Star Vega and the Cowherd Star Altair, who cross the Milky Way to meet once a year on this evening. Prayers are offered to the two stars, asking for proficiency in sewing, calligraphy and handicraft work.

"Hozuki-Ichi"

The "Hozuki-ichi," or ground-cherry fair, is held at the Sensoji Temple in Asakusa, Tokyo for two days—July 9–10. The precinct and the main approaches to the temple are filled with shops and stalls selling ground-cherries. Every year, more than 300 shops are set up, selling a potted ground-cherry for about ¥1,200.

After purchase, the customer carefully extracts the contents of the fruit to make a shell leaving only a small hole at the top. Young girls usually chew this small balloon-shaped shell to make a squeaking noise.

It is believed that those who worship at the temple during those two days will have 46,000 days of good fortune.

"Bon" Festival

According to Buddhist belief, the spirits of the dead visit their families on earth during the "Bon" season. "Bon" is celebrated from July 13 to 16 in Tokyo and some parts of eastern Japan, and between Aug. 13 and 16 in the rural districts and many parts of western Japan. Religious services are held to comfort and welcome back the spirits of the departed. Buddhist priests visit various homes to read the sutra, and the family members make offerings of food and flowers. The festival is also known as the Feast of Lanterns because lanterns are used to light the way for the homecoming spirits.

"Bon Odori"

"Bon Odori" is a community dance performed at the time of "Bon." In the evenings, "Bon" dances are staged in shrine and temple compounds, and groups of "yukata" (light summer kimono with bold patterns)-clad men and women merrily join in. Especially famous and the most hilarious of the "Bon" dances is the Awa Odori of Tokushima City on Shikoku, where the entire city overflows with lively singing and dancing.

"Tsukimi"

"Tsukimi" or moon-viewing is enjoyed by many Japanese families, traditionally on the night of the 15th day of the eighth month by the lunar calendar (September the 8th by solar calendar), when the moon is believed to reach its maximum rotundity and brightness. Friends are invited to join in this delightful observance. Offerings are made to the moon of pampas grass, rice dumplings, and seasonal fruit and vegetables by placing them on tables set up on the veranda by the windows.

"Shichi-Go-San" Festival

November 15 is "Shichi-Go-San," or the "Seven-Five-Three Festival." On this day, girls of seven, boys of five, and three-year-old children of either sex are taken to local shrines by their parents. The idea is to express their thanks to the tutelary deities for having reached these critical ages, and also to pray for future blessings. Dressed in their Sunday best—with many of the girls wearing long-sleeved kimono, they usually pose for photographs in front of the shrine. They also make it a rule to buy what is called "chitose-ame" (1,000-year candy), a symbol of longevity, at the stalls set up in the shrine precincts.

"Tori-no-Ichi"

"Tori-no-ichi," or cock fairs, are held at the various Otori Shrines in Tokyo, the most famous of which is located in downtown Asakusa. These fairs take place on the "cock" days in November according to the Oriental zodiac calendar (cf. p. 84). The main feature of the fairs is the sale of "kumade," bamboo rakes decorated with various trinkets, at the roadside stalls around the shrines. "Kumade" come in all sizes and in a wide range of prices, the largest and most elaborately decorated rake running into tens of thousands of yen. Used for decorating household altars, "kumade" are supposed to rake in good fortune and prosperity during the coming year.

"Hari-Kuyo"

In olden times, needle workers sewing clothes took a day off on the 8th of every month. On Dec. 8 a typical "Hari-kuyo," or memorial service of old broken and rusty needles, is observed at Awashima-do, a small temple located in the precincts of the Sensoji Temple in Asakusa, Tokyo. The discarded needles are stuck into soft "tofu" (bean curd) by the people who once used them as a sort of memorial, with those assembled there praying for the repose of the worn-out needles. "Kuyo" stands for memorial service.

"O-Misoka"—the Grand Last Day

The last day of each month is called "misoka," which literally means "the 30th day." Dec. 31, however, is specially referred to as "O-Misoka," or the grand last day. On this day, Japanese people give their houses a particularly thorough cleaning. Afterwards, they eat a bowl of noodles—a symbol of longevity—and then sit up till midnight to listen to the 108 peals of the temple bells. In the meantime, radio and TV stations broadcast special "O-Misoka" programs, which range from shows several hours long presenting a galaxy of popular singers to the performance of Beethoven's Ninth Symphony.

"Joya-no-Kane"

At midnight on New Year's Eve, every temple bell in Japan is struck 108 times to ring out the old year and ring in the new. This custom is based on the Buddhist idea that man has 108 worldly cares. Incidentally, the rosaries used by Buddhist believers have 108 beads. In this age of radio and television, people not only can listen to the peals of celebrated and historic bells in all parts of Japan, but also watch the once-mystic rites of ringing the "Joya-no-Kane" while sitting in the comfort of their own homes.

"Tori-no-ichi"

FESTIVALS

Grass-burning

Grass-burning on Wakasukayama Hill in Nara takes place on Jan. 15. Toward evening the priests of the Todaiji and Kofukuji Temples gather at a Shinto shrine at the foot of Wakakusayama Hill and hold a religious ceremony. At 6:30 p.m., the priests start fires on the hill at a signal from trumpets and a fireworks display. All the grass covering some 330 ha. of land on the hill is burnt off within an hour. The grass on the hill is set ablaze to destroy the habitat of birds and insects that damage crops in the neighborhood.

Snow Festival

Snow Festival or "Yuki-matsuri" in Sapporo, held for a couple of days in late January or early February, now ranks first among the annual events in Hokkaido. It features the elaborately sculptured snow images displayed on Odori Park in the city center and at Makomanai in the suburbs. Figures and structures built of snow and ice vary in size and subject. Some are based on legends and stories for children, while others are inspired by current events. Featuring a variety of gala events and entertainments, the Snow Festival attracts millions of visitors every year.

"Kamakura"

"Kamakura," an annual festival in Yokote City in northern Japan, is held on Feb. 15–16. In this singular event peculiar to the snowy north, children of the district build round snow huts resembling the igloos of Eskimos. Usually built along the city's side streets, they are known by the name of "kamakura." In these "kamakura" the children set up Shinto shrine altars dedicated to the God of Water, decorating them with offerings of food and flowers. In the evening, the "kamakura" are all lighted and the children spend a pleasant time there, chatting around the cozy braziers placed inside these unique snow huts. Both the children and passers-by are served a sweet drink called "amazake" fermented from "sake."

Eyo Festival

The Eyo Festival of the Saidaiji Temple in Saidaiji, Okayama Prefecture, is celebrated on the third Saturday night in February. It is popularly known by the name of "Hadaka Matsuri," or nude festival, because the young men taking part in it are nude except for small loin cloths. This manly festival has had a reputation for being one of Japan's three most strange festivals ever since it originated in the 10th century. At 8 p.m. on festival day, a drum beat signals the start of the festivities. All of the participants purify themselves in the water of the Yoshii River, then at mid-night they rush into the temple grounds to catch a pair of sacred wands thrown from above by the temple priest.

"Nagashibina"

"Nagashibina," or doll-floating ceremony, is widely observed in the rural districts of Tottori Prefecture. Nowadays, this ceremony is held at Mochigase-cho in March (lunar calendar), attracting a large number of visitors to the town. It originated in the Muromachi period (1336–1573) and is celebrated by people to protect them against calamity. At first, people place "hina" dolls, made of clay and papier-mache, on the altars along with an offering of food and white wine. After a solemn Shinto rite, they carry these dolls to a river and set them afloat. The dolls are supposed to carry away with them all of the town's evils.

Aoi Matsuri

Aoi Matsuri in Kyoto is the annual festival of Kamikamo and Shimokamo Shrines. It is held on May 15 and is highlighted by a colorful procession recreating the ancient parade of Imperial courtiers. The name of the festival derives from the fact that "aoi" (hollyhock) leaves are used in decorating the costumes of the paraders as well as the ox-drawn Imperial carriage. Clad in the costumes of the Heian period (794–1192), people in the procession parade with the carriage to the Shimokamo and Kamikamo Shrines. The procession starts at 10 a.m. from the plaza of the Kyoto Imperial Palace, winds its way to the Shimokamo Shrine and then disbands at the Kamikamo Shrine after the paraders perform a Shinto ceremony there.

Hakata Yamagasa

Hakata Yamagasa Matsuri in Fukuoka city, Kyushu, takes
place annually July 1–15, highlighted by a stirring parade
of decorative floats popularly known as "yama." The
"yama," usually 6 to 7.5 m. high, weighing 1,000 kg., are
colorfully decked with elaborate dolls made by the city's
well-known Hakata dollmakers. The spectacular floats
parade through the main street of the city on July 12, 13
and 15. The procession on the last day has a special name,
"Oiyama," or the chase of the floats. With the beating of
a large drum at 4.59 a.m. on the dot the first float starts
racing down the streets, with each of five-minute intervals,
chasing the ones ahead of it.

Gion Matsuri

Gion Matsuri in Kyoto, which takes place annually from
July 1 to 29 in honor of the Yasaka Shrine, is regarded
as one of the most important festivals in the ancient capital.
It features a grand parade of decorative floats on July 17.
The procession is composed of 20 floats, all decorated with
the elaborate works of present-day artisans.

There are two kinds of floats—the "yama" and the
"hoko." The "yama" is carried on the shoulders of several
men by means of long poles, while the "hoko," which has
wheels and is topped by 26-m.-high mast, is drawn by a
group of youths. The procession of the "yama" and "hoko"
starts from Shijo Karasuma Street at 9 a.m. on July 17,
and winds through the main streets in downtown Kyoto
until around 11 a.m.

Nomaoi Matsuri

Nomaoi Matsuri, or wild horse chase, at Soma City, in
Fukushima Prefecture takes place July 23–25. It is highlighted by a grand parade of horsemen clad in feudal

Nomaoi Matsuri

"samurai" (warrior) costumes. The festival can be traced back to military training conducted by Masakado Taira, the ancestor of the Somas—the feudal lord of the province.

The festival reaches its climax on July 24, when the armed horsemen vie with one another in attempting to catch shrine flags shot up into the air at a signal from a fireworks display.

The wild horse chase is staged on July 25—the last day of the festival. In this ceremony, men dressed in white try to mount with their bare hands, bare-backed horses chased into an enclosure by the horsemen.

"Rendai-Watashi"

The "Rendai-watashi" Festival takes place on the Oi River in Shizuoka Prefecture in late-July. The exact date of the festival is usually announced just before it is held. It recreates the way the Oi River was crossed in the Edo period (1603–1867). People used to cross the river on someone's shoulders or by means of a ferry litter called "rendai," which is borne on the shoulders of several sturdy men.

The "Rendai-watashi" Festival features the colorful rivercrossing of a "daimyo" (feudal lord) procession, consisting of 10 litters. His retainers cross on each other's shoulders.

Nebuta Matsuri

The Nebuta Matsuri in Aomori City, the capital of Aomori Prefecture, is celebrated from Aug. 3 to 7. It is included among the three most famous summer festivals in northern Japan, the other two being the Tanabata Matsuri in Sendai and the Kanto Matsuri in Akita.

The "nebuta" is a huge float dominated by a massive papier-mache dummy of a legendary hero or popular character from a children's story. It is pulled by many men wearing the colorful costumes peculiar to the festival. Gaily lighted in the evening, dozens of these "nebuta" parade through the street accompanied by hundreds of persons dressed up to suit their own fancy.

Kanto Festival

The Kanto Festival of Akita City in Akita Prefecture takes place Aug. 3–7. The "kanto" is a long 12-m.-high bamboo pole with nine bamboo bars, each of which is hung with 24 to 48 lanterns, according to the length of the pole. Measuring about 8 m. in height and weighing 45 to 60 kg., they are carried on the shoulders of stout youths. The "kanto" supposedly represents a rice plant in all its ripeness, and the festival is held to invoke divine help for a rich harvest.

"Mandoro"

"Mandoro," the lantern-lighting rite of the Kasuga Shrine in Nara, is one of the most popular ceremonies staged in the ancient capital of Nara. Some 3,000 or more lanterns of the Kasuga Shrine are lighted all at once on the evening of Aug. 15, presenting a dramatically colorful sight.

About half of these lanterns line the approach to the shrine, while the remainder are hung from the eaves of the shrine buildings. The Kasuga Shrine was founded in 768 and is beautifully painted in vermillion. Situated in the midst of a thick grove of trees the shrine retains the atmosphere of its ancient days.

"Daimonji-yaki"

"Daimonji-yaki," or the Great Bonfire, held on August 16 in Kyoto, is a spectacular summer event. Of the five bonfires lighted in Kyoto, the Daimonji on the 466-m.-high Mt. Nyoigatake is the most famous.

This festival derives from a Buddhist observance in which people express hope that their departed family members will find their way back to heaven. The bonfire on Mt. Nyoigatake is lighted in the shape of Chinese character   (dai), meaning "large." The horizontal stroke is 76-m.-long and the other two measure 136 m. and 170 m. respectively. The bonfires in Kyoto are lighted one after the other around 8 p.m., each one burning for about 40 minutes. Similar bonfires are burnt on the same day on Mt. Myojogatake at Hakone.

"Yabusame"

"Yabusame," or horseback archery, of the Tsurugaoka Hachimangu Shrine in Kamakura takes place on Sept. 16. It is the highlight of the annual festival of the Hachimangu Shrine, which is celebrated on September 15 and 16.

"Yabusame" is actually a contest among archers on horseback reproducing the training of "samurai" (warrior) in the Kamakura period (1192–1333).

Men on horseback wearing ancient "samurai" costumes compete with one another in shooting at wooden targets set up along a special course in the shrine precincts.

"Sennin-gyoretsu"

"Sennin-gyoretsu," or the procession of 1,000 men, takes place in Nikko on May 18 and Oct. 17 during the Grand Festival of the Toshogu Shrine dedicated to the first Tokugawa Shogun Ieyasu (1542–1616).

A thousand men dressed in the costumes of warriors and priests participate in the "sennin-gyoretsu," the highlight of the festival.

The 1,000-man procession, including three Shinto shrine palanquins (portable shrines), starts at 11 a.m. from the Futarasan Shrine and proceeeds to the Otabisho (place of sojourn for Shinto deities) near the Shinkyo (Sacred Bridge). Ritual Shinto dances are performed at the Otabisho, after which the procession returns to the Toshogu Shrine in the afternoon.

Jidai Matsuri

Jidai Matsuri on Oct. 22 is one of the most famous festivals in Kyoto. The annual function of the Heian Shrine, it was started in 1895 in honor of Emperor Kammu (737–806). The Jidai Matsuri (lit. Era Festival) is highlighted by a unique procession of several groups of people dressed in colorful costumes. Each group represents a period in the history of more than 11 centuries since the founding of the old capital in 794 by the Emperor Kammu.

The procession starts from the Kyoto Imperial Palace at around noon and reaches the Heian Shrine at 2:30 p.m. after winding through the main streets of Kyoto.

"Namahage"

"Namahage" of Oga Peninsula, Akita Prefecture, is a

singular event annually observed on Dec. 31. It originated from a legend about a Chinese emperor of Ham who landed in this part of Japan with five demons (probably powerful warriors). The emperor worked those demons hard every day of the year, except on January 15 when the demons were allowed to go to the villages and do what they wanted.

The "Namahage" features a visit to each home in the village by a group of four or five men disguised as demons and armed with kitchen knives and similar articles. All single young men assemble at the Akagami Shrine in the evening and form into several groups. After participating in a Shinto ceremony there, they start their march toward the village and make the rounds of the allotted areas.

"Namahage"

RELIGION

Shinto

Shinto (lit. the way of the gods) is the native religion of Japan, originating from primitive ancestor- and nature-worship. It has no Bible or dogmas like Christianity.

Its pantheon includes deities that are the personifications of natural phenomena as well as great leaders and heros of the past. Thus, Shinto is polytheistic. Beginning from Amaterasu Omikami, Goddess of the Sun, and many other mythological deities from the dawn of the nation and proceeding down to numerous deities created in each succeeding period, Shinto has ended up with "myriads of gods and deities."

Whereas the Shinto gods originating in Japan's pre-historic times are all mythological beings, the later deities are all actual beings—historical persons such as emperors, great warriors and even scholars, who have been deified posthumously and added to the Shinto pantheon.

"Jinja" or Shrines

"Jinja" or Shinto shrines are sacred to various deities, but the most common are the "temmangu," "hachimangu" and "inari" shrines.

"Temmangu" Shrine The "temmangu" is consecrated in honor of Michizane Sugawara, a scholar-statesman in the latter part of the 9th century. The main "temmangu" shrines are at Dazaifu in Kyushu and Kitano in Kyoto. As it is dedicated to the "God of Learning," the "temmangu" is visited by a large number of students during the spring exam season.

"Hachiman" Shrine "Hachiman" shrine is dedicated to Emperor Ojin, Empress Jingu and the obscure Hime Okami. Later, the militaristic Genji, or Minamoto clan began to worship "hachiman" as its tutelary god; Yoritomo, the leader of the clan, set up a military administration in Kamakura in 1192, erecting a "hachiman" shrine at Tsurugaoka. "Hachiman" then began to be worshipped as the God of War.

"Inari" Shrine The original "inari" shrine is at Fushimi in Kyoto, although there are more than 30,000 "inari" shrines scattered throughout the country. At first, the shrine was sacred to the Goddess of Rice and Cereals, but with the rise of commerce and industry, "inari" began to be worshipped as the God of Good Fortune. The shrine is guarded by two foxes, messengers of the God, to whom custom requires that "aburage" (pieces of fried bean curd) be offered. Hence, the name of "inari-zushi" (fried bean curd stuffed with vinegared rice).

"Torii"

"Torii" (lit. a perch for birds) is a gateway formed by two upright and two horizontal beams. It stands in front of every Shinto shrine or marks its approach.

In the case of Hakone Shrine in the scenic resort area of the same name, the "torii" stands in the lake, while the famous red-orange "torii" of Itsukushima Shrine on Miyajima Island near Hiroshima stands in the sea. Sometimes a long, seemingly endless avenue of "torii" can be found like those at "inari" shrine. The usual material is wood or stone, but "torii" of concrete, copper or even porcelain can occasionally be seen. The various "torii" styles cannot be counted on the fingers of both hands.

"Komainu"

"Komainu" (lit. Korean dog) are actually lion-shaped images squatting in pairs in front of Shinto shrines. They are designed to create an impression of pomp and dignity as well as ward off evil spirits.

It is believed that originally the pair consisted of a lion stationed on the left and a dog on the right. With the passage of time, however, the distinction gradually disappeared, with the dog gaining prominence over the lion.

"Komainu" are variegated in shape: some have horns and others are open mouthed, while the pair does not always consist of the same animal. Some say that open-mouthed image on the left represents a lion and the horned tight lipped one on the right dog. "Komainu" are not confined to Shinto shrines. In fact, very few Buddhist temples are guarded by the pair.

"Shimenawa"

"Shimenawa" (lit. a rope of occupancy) is stretched before the abode of a Shinto god to prevent the intrusion of defiled things. The rope is made of rice straw and is adorned with many straws and paper hangings.

Not only the abode of a god, but the household altar is also marked off with this sacred rope. During the New Year's season, the gateway or entrance of most Japanese homes is decorated with this rope, among other things. The famous twin rocks offshore at Futamigaura near the Grand Shrines of Ise are joined by a large straw rope. Thus "shimenawa" signifies the abode of holy beings. This same stout hemp rope with its "gohei" paper hanging is worn by the grand champions of sumo wrestling when they make their daily ceremonial entry into the ring during tournaments. It's not called by the same name, but signifies holiness all the same.

"Ema"

"Ema" is a votive picture tablet offered in prayer or out of a sense of gratitude to a Shinto shrine or a Buddhist temple. The tablet, the upper part of which is shaped like a roof, once bore a picture of a horse since it was offered in lieu of a horse; hence, the name (pictorial horse).

Nowadays, however, the pictures represent a thousand and one things. For example, a man who has sore eyes may paint a picture of eyes in the hope that he will get well.

"Gohei"

"Gohei" (lit. a bundle of cloth), made of white, silver or gold colored paper strips dangling from a stick, is offered to Shinto deities. They represent the offerings of cloth tied to branches of the sacred cleyera tree in ancient times.

This wand of white paper strips waved by the

officiating Shinto priest at prayers is supposed to invite the descent of the gods and ward off evil. Even today a Shinto priest is invited to wave "gohei" on such happy occasions as weddings, births, ground-breakings and the completion of buildings.

"Shichi Fukujin"

Just as Westerners have their Three Furies, so too the Japanese have their "Seven Deities of Luck" (Shichi Fukujin), who preside over their earthly bliss. The deities are "Ebisu" (God of Fishermen and Trademen), "Daikoku" (God of Farmers), "Benten" or "Benzaiten" (Goddess of Eloquence, Music, Wisdom and Wealth), "Bishamon" (God of Warriors and Protector of Buddhism), "Fukurokuju" (God of Prophets), "Jurojin" (God of Longevity) and "Hotei" (God of Open-mindedness and Wealth).

Of the seven, "Benten" is the only member of the fair sex. In fact, the word "Benten" a synonym for a beauty was in popular parlance. "Benten" at Enoshima appears as a nude god holding a lute, while "Benten" in Kamakura is called "Zeniarai (money cleansing) Benten" because of the folk belief that anybody who cleanses his money in the spring water of the Benten Shrine will see it doubled later on.

"Konsei-sama"

The cult of phallicism in Japan is represented by the worship of "Konsei-sama," a god in the form of a phallus of natural stone or wood. Supplication is made to "Konsei-sama" for a happy marriage or successful conception. The custom requires that the votary make an offering of a small metal, stone or wood phallus. At Konsei Pass in the interior part of Nikko area there is a small and very old shrine dedicated to this god.

"Omamori"

"Omamori" (amulets) are paper, cloth or wood tablets mainly conferred by Shinto shrines. They are handmade by Shinto priests and consecrated by prayers before the deities. The recipients wear or keep them in a suitable place in the home to ward off evil or to invite good fortune. If you ride in a cab or bus very often, you may occasionally notice a talisman for traffic safety stuck on the panel in front of the driver's seat.

"Omikuji"

"Omikuji" (a written oracle) is drawn at Shinto shrines to learn of the divine will or to read one's star. The oracle thus given is divided into good and bad luck, with several intermediate stages. People seek thereby to tell their fortune in money matters, marriage, the right direction in which they should travel, etc.

After reading their fortune, they tie their "omikuji" onto the branches of a tree standing in the shrine precincts, praying for the materialization of the good luck they have drawn or for the banishment of the bad luck. At some Shinto shrines popular for fortune-telling, the tree bearing dozens of "omikuji" looks as if it were blooming with a multitude of white flowers.

"Ennichi"

"Ennichi" (lit. communion day) originally meant the day when living beings held communion with the Buddha and other Buddhist deities.

When large crowds of people were attracted to a shrine or a temple on such a day, merchants set up stalls in front of the temple to sell their wares. Eventually, some of these stalls developed into permanent stores and a town grew up around the shrine or the temple.

Nowadays, the term denotes a fair held in the evening in front of or even within the precincts of a Buddhist temple or Shinto shrine on a certain fixed date. The "Hozuki-ichi" (ground-cherry fair), which takes place at the Sensoji Temple (Kannon Temple) at Asakusa, Tokyo, on July 9-10, is one of the most popular "ennichi" in Tokyo, redolent of the old Edo atmosphere.

"Mikoshi"

"Mikoshi" (shrine palanquin or portable shrine) is used when the emblem of a Shinto deity travels from the main shrine to another shrine, or vice versa. Patterned after the emperor's palanquin, it consists of three parts—platform, body and roof, with the body symbolizing the deity's original shrine. Most of the portable shrines are made of wood, lacquered in black and gilded.

At Shinto shrine festivals, youths (including some girls nowadays) dressed in "happi" coats bear portable shrines on their shoulders, loudly crying: "wasshoi, wasshoi" reminiscent of the turbulent days of the latter Heian period (794-1192) when warrior-monks painted the town red in an effort to push through their demands. Sometimes portable shrines are carried into a river or the sea for purification or similar purpose.

"Mikoshi"

"Dashi"

Along with "mikoshi" (portable shrine), "dashi" (floats) play an indispensable part in Shinto shrine festivals. The floats are colorfully decorated with flowers and branches as well as dolls representing men, birds and animals. Musical bands of flutes, drums, gongs and other instruments often perform on the floats as they parade down the street. Among the festivals noted for their gorgeously decorated floats are the Gion Matsuri of the Yasaka Shrine in Kyoto, Sanno Matsuri at Takayama in Gifu Prefecture and the Night Festival at Chichibu in Saitama Prefecture.

Buddhism

Buddhism Buddhism is a religion that originated in India by the Buddha (Gautama), who was born in 653 B.C. It does not preach any particular dogmas or doctrines, but teaches the way to self-perfection and aims at solving various problems of life. Knowledge or enlightenment is the condition of Buddhist grace.

Buddhism was introduced into Japan in 538 A.D. Since then, it has exerted a profound influence on the spiritual life and culture of the Japanese people.

In Japan, however, Buddhism has become more secular, concerning itself, for instance, with ancestor worship and prayers for bountiful crops—a far cry from its original philosophic concept founded in India. At present, as indicated by such a phrase as the "funeral bonze" uttered by a carping tongue, the main tasks assigned to Buddhism are to take charge of funeral rites and say mass for the dead.

Shintoism, on the other hand, officiates on happy occasions—at weddings, births, and the beginning and completion of construction projects.

Buddhist Sects Since Buddhism in its inception had no definite dogmas—knowledge or enlightment being the sole means of salvation—it was only natural that Buddhism should have been divided into numerous sects before it reached Japan.

The main sects still extant are the Tendai, Shingon (esoteric), Jodo and Zen (Rinzai, Soto and other subsects) and the Jodo Shin-shu and Nichiren sects.

Since World War II, new religious organizations have come to exercise strong influences on the masses, throwing into the shade the time-honored Buddhist sects.

Zen Sect   Zen (the meditation sect of Buddhism) put immense importance on free will and salvation through self-help to the extent of denying the merit of the Buddha in interceding. In fact, it consists in the active practice of pious meditation to attain direct intuitive insights into noumena.

In the feudal age, Zen was practiced by the "samurai" (warrior) class as an aid to their mental discipline. It formed the cardinal principles of the tea ceremony and the flower arrangement as well as of other traditional arts such as "sumi-e" (landscape painting done in carbon ink) and landscape garden design, to mention a few. Thus, it has exerted a profound influence on the thought and culture of the Japanese people.

"Za-zen"

"Za-zen" (sitting Zen, or practice of meditation) is a way of training one's mind so as to attain enlightenment. The proper method and procedures as well as the spirit of "za-zen" were first taught in Japan by Dogen (1200–1253), who brought the Soto sect approach to Zen Buddhism back from China.

"Za-zen," like Yoga, requires one to squat with the legs crossed, to relax the mind and to enter into a frame of mind emptied of all ideas and thoughts. In order to be faithful to the teaching of the Buddha that "there is nothing to rely on but yourself to attain salvation," in Zen meditation you are advised to have the conviction that "you yourself are a Buddha, which you will prove by "za-zen." The three essentials of "za-zen" are said to be "sitting straight, putting force on the navel and regulating respiration."

"Ji-In (Tera)" or Temple

Buddhist temples are called "ji-in" or "tera." Nowadays, however, the tendency is for people to visit their precincts more to imbibe the quiet atmosphere, to say nothing of the architectural and artistical aesthetic beauty they provide, than the worship, which is done in passing, so to speak. Youths, particularly young women, seem to have a great liking for ancient Buddhist temples, and not a few of them profess that making pilgrimages to Buddhist temples is one of their hobbies. Such is not the case, however, with the Shinto shrines.

"Shukubo"

The term "shukubo" means, among other things, a temple abode where the faithful may put up for the night. In these days of universal tourism, there is a growing tendency among tourists to use "shukubo" as a low-priced inn. Guests are not necessarily requested to attend a religious service, but at the Eiheiji Temple near Fukui City, the head temple of the Soto sect of Zen Buddhism, laymen are asked to get up about 4 a.m. and join the monks in the practice of meditation—"za-zen."

"Shojin Ryori" (Vegetable Diet)

Buddhism puts faith in rebirth by karma, and thus prohibits any destruction of life. It also extols frugal meals as a way to enlightenment, admonishing monks against lavish meals. Thus, Buddhist monks have evolved a culinary art of their own, concentrating on vegetables and seaweed, and shunning the flesh of fish, fowls and animals. Such cooking is called in Japan "shojin ryori."

In the secular world, too, a custom emerged of taking "shojin ryori" for a certain period before and after the anniversary of the death of relatives and ancestors.

On the other hand, as a result of the development of tourism, some Buddhist temples have begun serving "shojin ryori" in restaurant-style to visitors. Such meals are gaining popularity, thanks to the growing interest in dietetics. Because of the popularity as well as of the convenience of the serving temple, which is not a restaurant, a reservation several days in advance is required when taking such a meal at a Buddhist temple.

"Junrei" or Pilgrimage

"Junrei" means a pilgrimage to Buddhist holy places for salvation. The word also means a pilgrim.

The oldest pilgrimage route was laid out on Shikoku Island consisting of 88 holy places. The length of the route totals 1,300 km. and requires two months to

Pilgrims

cover on foot. Originally, the use of any kind of vehicle or horse was taboo, but nowadays many pilgrims take trains and buses to cover the entire route, which takes 20–25 days. In addition, "a pilgrim bus tour" is available and takes about two weeks.

The pilgrim proceeds on foot, ringing a small hand-bell, singing hymns and asking for alms of rice or money from families along the road. The custom of providing a pilgrim with free lodging (charity lodging) is still observed in some places in and around Shikoku.

Similar pilgrimages to holy places have since developed in many other districts around Japan. In the neighborhood of Tokyo, for instance, a pilgrimage route to 34 holy places in Chichibu, Saitama Prefecture has been organized.

"Aragyo" or Religious Austerities

In order to realize a religious truth or to attain a higher perception of reality, Buddhist monks undergo rigorous mental and physical training. The physical austerities they practice are called "aragyo," which include, among other things, fasting for many days, hours of exposure to freezing waters under a waterfall during the coldest season, etc. One certain sect requires its monks to walk in bare feet on burning embers and even on the sharp edge of a sword. By practicing such superman austerities, Buddhist monks try to achieve their transformation into holy beings different from the laity.

Buddhist Statues

Statues of Buddha first appeared around the end of the first century. They are divided into four types—the images of the "Nyorai," "Bosatsu," "Myoo" and the "Tembu."

"Nyorai" The word "Nyorai" means completeness, and the "Nyorai" Buddha is represented by those who have attained enlightenment or perceived the ultimate truth of the universe.

"Bosatsu" The "Bosatsu" (Bodhisattva), meaning the Buddhas who are in pursuit of truth, includes many Buddhas under this name—"Kanzeon Bosatsu," "Jizo Bosatsu," "Fugen Bosatsu" and "Monju Bosatsu." The "Bosatsu" is an assistant or attendant to the "Nyorai." He will show mercy to anyone who asks a favor of him. As "Kanzeon Bosatsu" or Kannon (Goddess of Mercy) is the most popular Buddha with the public, there are many temples in Japan in which its statues are enshrined. The "Jizo Bosatus" is a guardian of children and its stone image characterized by a clean-shaven head, is often found along the country roadsides.

"Myoo" The "Myoo" (Vidyaraja) is represented by "Fudo Myoo" (Avalanathah), which is a popular Buddhist divinity worshipped by many people. It has a fierce mien, with flames shooting up from its back. The "Fudo Myoo" is an incarnation of the "Nyorai" who have appeared in this world to preach down those unwilling to embrace the Buddhist faith. The "Nio" (Deva King) is also popular with the public. Regarded as guardians of temple gates its statues can be found in the niches on either side of the gate.

"Tembu" The "Tembu," or Heavenly Gods, are divided into two groups. The first group includes the "Bishamon-ten," "Taishakuten" and "Juni-Shinsho", all of which are clad in Chinese-style armor. The other group, including the "Kichijoten," "Bonten," "Gigeiten," "Benzaiten" and others, are all female and wear heavenly robes.

Pagodas

The five-story pagoda ("goju-no-to") containing the ashes of the Buddha in its basement, is a symbol and the most conspicuous building within the compound of a Buddhist monastery. Its five roofs represent the five elements of earth, water, fire, wind and air. Originally, it was erected to indicate a holy place, but since the latter part of the Heian period (794–1192), the pagoda has been erected to add to the pomp and splendor of a Buddhist monastery.

Among the more famous five-story pagodas are those

at the Horyuji Temple near Nara (34.1 m. high), the Muroji Temple also near Nara (16.18 m.), the Kofukuji Temple in Nara (50 m.) and the Toji Temple in Kyoto (36 m.).

"Tsurigane" or Hanging Bell

"Tsurigane" or hanging bell of a Buddhist temple is believed to have followed in the wake of Buddhism. Japan's oldest extant temple bell (national treasure), cast in 689, hangs in the belfry of the Myoshinji Temple in Kyoto.

Temple bells were originally intended to report the hours, but gradually they gained religious meaning, as witness the use of the bell to toll out the old year with 108 strokes (dispelling 108 "worldly passions").

The largest temple bell of its kind in Japan is that of Chion-in Temple in Kyoto, measuring 2.7 m. in diameter, 5.4 m. in height and 74 short tons in weight.

The bell of the Miidera on the shores of Lake Biwa (celebrated for its melodious sound), the Byodo-in bell at Uji near Kyoto (noted for its graceful shape) and the Jingoji bell at Takao, Kyoto, (bearing an inscription by Toshiyuki Fujiwara of calligraphic fame) are regarded as Japan's three most famous temple bells.

"Mokugyo"

"Mokugyo" (lit. wooden fish) is a gong sounded in a Buddhist temple to signal that it's time for sutra chanting. It has a round, fish-like shape, with its surface carved into fish scales. As it is believed that fish keep their eyes open day and night, the wooden "fish gong" serves

"Mokugyo"

a warning to the bonzes against laziness and idle slumber. To the layman, however, its sound ("poku, poku") is, in contrast to the solemn and sonorous sound of the temple bell, so dull and monotonous that it seems more like it's enticing the monks to the Land of Nod than to meditation.

"Shimbutsu Kongo"

"Shimbutsu kongo" literally means mixture of Shinto gods and Buddhas. Sometime after the introduction of Buddhism into Japan from the Asiatic continent, attempts were made to reconcile native Shinto gods with the Buddhist deities. This trend continued until the Meiji Restoration (1868), when the two religions were separated for good and all.

The Jingoji Temple in Kyoto, for instance, stood within the precincts of a Shinto shrine, and it was not rare for Buddhist temples and Shinto shrines to stand side by side. The Toyokawa Inari, one of the three greatest "inari" shrines, is also called the Myogonji Temple (of the Soto sect of Zen Buddhism). Although it is a Buddhist temple, it has a "torii" gate in its precincts.

Even today, many Japanese people worship at both Shinto and Buddhist altars at the same time, revealing their unique ability to assimilate two or more religious beliefs at the same time without experiencing a sense of apparent conflict.

Christianity in Japan

Christianity was first introduced into Japan in 1549 when Francis Xavier, a Spanish Jesuit missionary, landed at Kagoshima. From that time until 1639—the year in which the last of the missionaries were expelled, Roman Catholic missionaries were active in Japan. Favored at first for the opportunities they provided for foreign trade, Christian missionaries were later placed under a ban by Hideyoshi Toyotomi (1536–1598) for fear of Japan's being colonized by Spain or Portugal. When the Tokugawa shogunate was established in 1603, still stricter measures were adopted. It was in 1873, five years after the Meiji Restoration, that the doors were reopened to Christian missionaries.

At present, Japanese followers of Christ total about 1.1 million—nearly one percent of the total population, including about 730,000 Protestants and 370,000 Catholics.

"Kakure Kirishitan" or Hidden Christians

Some of the Japanese Christians, particularly those in Kyushu, who suffered intense persecution after the Shimabara Rebellion, or Amakusa "Kirishitan Revolt" (1637), kept their faith secretly by taking refuge in inaccessible rustic communities deep in the mountains or on small, remote isles. In fact, they went underground. Even today, their descendants can be found in western Kyushu.

Their religion is actually a rather peculiar folk belief, a mixture of Christianity with Shintoism and Buddhism as well as ancestor worship. The faithful do not belong to a Christian church, but keep icons secreted in their small household Buddhist shrines or Shinto "god-shelves." It is believed that their forebears professed a belief in Shintoism or Buddhism to conceal their true faith, and with the passage of time, the three faiths have merged into an unidentifiable form of religion.

A five-story pagoda of Muroji Temple

FOOD AND DRINKS

Japanese Food

Japanese food may perhaps be best described as the traditional products of no one except the Japanese people, with much emphasis on all the delicate shades of color, season and taste. Substantial nourishment seems to yield to eye-catching refinement that includes a bit of everything rather than a lump of meat. Such bloody material as beef is taboo; instead, marine products and vegetables are apt to play a leading role. It sometimes happens that a foreigner gets hungry for another meal a couple of hours after having Japanese food, but the real essence lies not in quantity but in quality.

Seasonings

"Miso" "Miso," or bean paste, a typically Japanese-style seasoning agent, is made of steamed soy bean fermented with a specific yeast mold bred in rice, barley or soy bean itself. "Miso" soup is one of the "musts" on the average Japanese breakfast table. Besides, "miso" is now being used for a wider variety of purposes. For instance, "miso" added to Chinese noodles is becoming popular.

"Shoyu" "Shoyu," or soy sauce, is a typical Japanese-style seasoning and is now sold throughout most of the world. Basically, it is made of wheat and soy bean, and technically these are mixed with a special yeast in concentrated salt water and then fermented for a long time. There are both natural and chemical brews, the former being classified into "strong" and "weak." It is indispensable for Japanese dishes.

Vinegar The Japanese word for vinegar is simply "su." Vinegar is often used in Japanese cooking. For example, the steamed rice for "sushi" must be delicately treated with vinegar first. "Su-no-mono," or vinegared dishes, are very popular and are often served as a kind of appetizer for Japanese food.

"Katsuobushi" "Katsuobushi," meaning dried bonito, is mainly used to create the delicate taste of Japanese clear soup. As it is hard as a rock, it is shaved with a special plane and its thin leaves are put in boiling water to make a soup base. As a matter of fact, this takes considerable time and labor, and an instant package of scraped "katsuobushi" can be obtained at any food market.

"Kaiseki Ryori"

This is rather formal food served at a fashionable, Japanese-style banquet. When this originated about 18th century, "kaiseki ryori" was connected with some special occasion such as a tea ceremony, but today its ceremonial background seems to have faded away. Commercialized in a sense, the menu is something like the Japanese version of a full-course dinner, including soup, "sashimi," broiled fish, boiled vegetables, and so on. The whole thing is served on a "kaiseki-zen," or a small individual table without legs.

"Sushi"

In making "sushi," rice is flavored with vinegar, salt and sugar, hand-molded into small ovals, covered with raw or cooked fish, shellfish or eggs, and sometimes rolled in dried seaweed called "nori." If you care to try fresh, authentic "sushi," sit at the counter of a "sushi" shop and order "sushi" piece by piece on the spot, although your bill will be much higher than otherwise. Good "sushi" is quite expensive, but real gourmets are not unduly bothered by the price.

"Sushi" restaurant

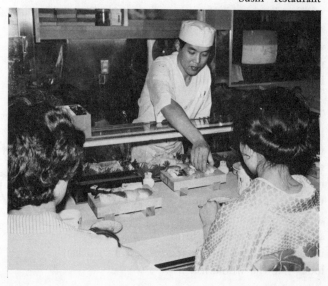

"Nori"

"Nori," or dried seaweed, is a daily breakfast favorite for a great many Japanese people. You toast it over a slow fire, break it in business card sized pieces and eat them with soy sauce and hot, steamed rice. Canned "nori," either toasted or untoasted is also available and is served as a very popular gift item of the "Bon" and year-end season together with Japanese green tea.

"Sashimi"

Many foreigners find such typical tastes as sukiyaki and tempura rather congenial, even when tasting them for the first time. But "sashimi," or raw, sliced fish, is perhaps an exception. Some foreigners might say: "Oh, it is the last thing I want to eat." However, others might insist: "Japanese food would not be nearly so fascinating without raw fish." True, no formal Japanese dinner party is complete without "sashimi." If you remain an anti-"sashimi" gourmet, you will also lose all the delicacies offered by "sushi," which is a varied combination of "sashimi" and steamed rice. For most Japanese families, the weekly dinner menu includes "sashimi" at least once.

"Ikizukuri"

"Ikizukuri" is a synonym for the very freshest "sashimi." In fact, the fish themselves are still alive at the time they are fillet-sliced, and even when they are eaten. The unique idea of "ikizukuri" is to make slices piece by piece to form its original shape so that it looks like the whole fish it

"Ikizukuri"

138

really is. Carp, red snapper and spiny lobster are often prepared this way.

"Odorigui"

Some may complain that it is cruel to eat something still alive, but cruel or not it is a popular practice in Fukuoka, Kyushu. The victim is a tiny creature called "shirauo," or whitebait. As several of these miniature fish swim around in a basin on a table, you scoop some of them up in a handy little net and eat them after dipping them in vinegar. The best season ranges between February and March. God bless the poor, tiny victims!

"Fugu" or Blowfish

"I love to eat blowfish, but dare not risk my life" is a popular Japanese counterpart of "Honey is sweet, but the bee stings." Blowfish is temptingly delicious, but is deadly poisonous, especially in its liver and ovaries. True epicureans treasure the most poisonous parts of the fish because the poison slightly benumbs their mouth, even though they are aware that giving in to such delicious temptation may actually cost them their lives. You do not necessarily have to be so adventurous. Blowfish, on the whole, are now completely safe when properly prepared by a licensed cook, and is popularly enjoyed as both "sashimi" and in "fugu-nabe"—a pot dish featuring blowfish meat, particularly during the best season between January and March.

"Tai" or Red Snapper

The Japanese red snapper is often considered as the "king of fish" both for its shape as well as its taste. Many Japanese immediately associate "tai" with "medetai"—something happy and auspicious. This is the reason why no Japanese food on some auspicious occasions can be complete without this particular fish. In most cases, "tai" is served as

139

"okashiratsuki," or whole fish broiled with salt, but it is also served as "sashimi."

"Unagi" or Eel

"Unagi," or eels, are widely considered to be an energizing food, even to the point where they are eaten on the mid-summer day called "doyo" so that one won't suffer from the prolonged summer heat. Eels are usually broiled over charcoal and served on rice or in lacquer boxes. Now it is necessary to either specially raise eels or import them. They are becoming so expensive with each passing year that many people say the "unagi" is a special dish they can afford only once a year around the time of the above-mentioned summer day.

Beef

Japanese beef claims to be the world's finest. This is no exaggeration for such special beef known as "Kobe beef" and "Matsuzaka beef." But it takes much more time and effort to produce beef of this quality. Fodder must be carefully selected, and sometimes the cattle are even fed beer and hand-massaged to ensure top-quality, tender and mel-low-tasting beef of a brilliant crimson color.

Sukiyaki

Sukiyaki is one of the typical Japanese dishes that usually appeal most to the foreign visitor's taste. Seasoned with "warishita" made from soy sauce, sukiyaki is a dish con-sisting of tender, thinly sliced beef, vegetables such as leeks, spinach and mushrooms, toasted bean curd and a gelatin-like ingredient called "konnyaku," or "shirataki." These ingre-dients are cooked in a saucepan over a gas burner in front of the guests and served to them piping hot.

"Shabu-Shabu"

"Shabu-shabu," originally an onomatopoeic word, is the

Japanese version of "do-it-yourself" cooking because you eat as you cook. Very thin slices of good-quality beef are a must. You pick up a piece with a pair of chopsticks and put it in the boiling water of the pan in the center of the table for just a few seconds. Then, remove it with the chopsticks, dip it in the seasoned soy sauce and eat it. A variety of vegetables and other ingredients are served along with the beef, while the broth left in the pan serves as a very good soup base for Japanese noodles at the climax of the "shabu-shabu" meal.

Tempura

Tempura consists of fish or vegetables dipped in batter and fried in deep fat. At fashionable tempura restaurants, tempura is prepared in front of the diners and served piping hot from the fryer. Tempura and sukiyaki are two of the most popular Japanese dishes with foreigners, although neither one is a traditional Japanese dish. Tempura is said to have been introduced by the Dutch, while sukiyaki dates back only a hundred years or so with the introduction of meat into Japanese diet by foreigners.

"Tofu"

"Tofu " or soybean curd, is made of vegetable protein and is greatly treasured in the diet of Japanese vegetarians. Actually, it is one of the most indispensable foods for the great majority of the Japanese people, who relish it in many diversified ways throughout the year.

The most popular and convenient ways of preparing it is using it as the basic ingredient of "miso" soup, as "hiyayakko" (chilled in ice cold water) in summer and adding it to "yudofu" (boiled in a pot) in winter. "Yakidofu " or toasted bean curd is a very popular ingredient in sukiyaki.

"Chawan-Mushi"

"Chawan-mushi" or steamed vegetable-and-meat custard, tastes both delicate and delicious. The cooking process is rather simple. Edible mushrooms, fruit of the gingko tree, chicken, sliced fish sausage and certain kinds of vegetable are mixed together and steamed in a covered, cup-like bowl until the egg base solidifies into a custard. "Chawan" means a bowl and "mushi" means to steam; hence, the name "chawan-mushi."

"Nabe-Ryori"

This literally means pot dishes—various dishes served in a wide-bottomed pot. You eat it as it cooks on a table, over a gas burner. Naturally, it is best enjoyed during the cold months. Practically everything can be put in the pot— chicken, oyster and fish, just as you desire. Blowfish meat makes a special feast, most ideally accompanied by Japanese "sake." "Chankonabe" is another type of this cooking, and serves as the daily fare for the Japanese professional sumo wrestlers. Some retired sumo wrestlers run "chankonabe" restaurants.

"Laomien" and Curried Rice

Among common everyday foods appealing to the ordinary Japanese, "laomien" and curried rice (curry rice in Japanese) are two most popular items. Restaurants serving one of these items or both are found almost everywhere through-out Japan. None of them are of Japanese origin. "Laomien" is Chinese, while curried rice Indian. Originally Chinese noodles, what is called "laomien" in Japan drastically adapted to suit the Japanese taste and no longer seems to be available in China—only in Japan. Curried rice is highly popular in Japan, too, and a variety of packaged, precooked curry snack are the best-selling items at supermarkets.

"Soba" and "Udon"

"Soba" and "udon" are two different types of Japanese noodles, "soba" being made from buckwheat flour and "udon" from wheat flour. These noodles are eaten from soup-filled bowls, or by dipping into specific soup. To find a noodle shop, just walk a block or two in any direction in town and you are bound to come across one with its familiar shop curtain called "noren." At many railway stations there is a small noodle stand, where passengers and commuters so deftly devour a bowl of noodles in a few minutes before the train leaves. When eating Japanese noodles, you can forget about Western manners since it is acceptable to make natural eating noises to slurp up the noodles if they really taste good.

"Sekihan"

"Sekihan" literally means "red rice," or actually rice boiled together with red beans. It is served as part of special feast for auspicious occasions, as many people believe that the red color is by nature happy and auspicious. Glutinous rice is used to make "sekihan," and it requires considerable skill to cook an ideal serving of red rice. Especially in big cities, therefore, home cooking is now on the decline as far as "sekihan" is concerned. Instead, more and more people are apt to get ready-made "sekihan" at nearby supermarkets or, uniquely enough, at Japanese-style confectionery shops.

"Ochazuke"

When you say you prefer something like "ochazuke," you either mean that your appetite is not very vigorous or that you are not very hungry at all. It is therefore synonymous with something small in amount and plain in taste. The recipe is quite simple, too. You pour very hot green tea over steamed rice served in a larger bowl than usual, accompanied by such popular side-dishes as broiled salted salmon, cod roe or pickled plum. A small dose of grated horseradish ("wasabi") will add a little spice. The best time to enjoy "ochazuke" is after a night of drinking.

Alcoholic Drinks

Japan is the home of top-grade whisky and beer, not to speak of Japanese "sake." There are innumerable brands of "sake" peculiar to each locality throughout the country. During the cold months, the majority of people like to drink hot "sake." It is also widely used as a seasoning agent in Japanese foods. Among Japanese beer, the "Kirin" brand enjoys a firm domestic market share of about 50%. On the other hand, Suntory and Nikka are among the most popular "Japanese Scotch whiskies."

Green Tea

Roughly speaking, there are three kinds of Japanese green tea (ranked in order of quality)—"gyokuro," "sencha" and "bancha." Quality is graded by the part of the tea leaves actually used as well as the method of processing. In Japan most tea is produced in Shizuoka and Uji on the outskirts of Kyoto. Tea was first introduced to Japan from China in the 12th century, and was used as a kind of medicine in the early days. Today, "let's have tea" actually means "let's take a short break," although coffee is usually predominant on such occasions. Green tea is offered at most restaurants—free of charge more often than not.

"Mugicha," or Barley Tea

This is a type of "tea" completely different from regular teas. It is made of barley and parched rather than refined. When you prepare "mugicha," you make a decoction of the barley in boiling water. In summer it tastes even more refreshing if served ice cold.

"Nabe-ryori"

SPORTS AND RECREATION

Baseball

Pro Baseball Pro baseball is no doubt one of the most popular sports in Japan attracting tens of millions of fans throughout the country. Just as in Major Leagues in the U.S., there are two different leagues here, too: the Central and Pacific—Japan's counterparts of the National and American Leagues. The pro baseball season extends between April and October, with the Japanese version of the World Series usually held in the latter parts of October. During the warm months, night games prevail so that more fans can go to their favorite ball parks or enjoy the games on television or radio free from their daily tasks.

High School Baseball Championship The All-Japan High School Baseball Tournament, with more than a 50-year history, is truly an exciting annual event at the height of the summer season in mid-August. Representing each prefectural area, some 50 high school teams converge on Koshien Stadium (located between Osaka and Kobe) after having survived a series of local elimination games involving more than 3,000 high schools altogether. They vie in a single elimination, pyramid-style tournament over a 10-day period under the scorching summer sun. Their refreshing ways appeal even to those who are not particularly interested in baseball. The tournament is so exciting that many people complain they cannot concentrate on their business until it's over.

Sumo

The history of Japanese sumo wrestling dates back to mythological times. Originally, it was a kind of divination rather than a sport. Even now we see some traces of this origin in the ceremonial ritual of sumo wrestlers. Sumo is the national sport of Japan, with six sumo tournaments being held annually—three in Tokyo (January, May and September), and one each in Osaka (March), Nagoya (July) and Fukuoka (November). A few foreign wrestlers are also official competitors, the most distinguished being Takamiyama, the heaviest wrestler of all at 165 kg. Hailing from Hawaii, Jesse Kuhaulua—his real name—enjoys the greatest popularity among foreign sumo fans.

Golf

Japan looks like a country of golf maniacs. There are more than 900 golf courses within its narrow confines, while the total golfing population is said to exceed 10 million. During the good seasons of spring and autumn, Japan attracts many top players from around the world because a series of financially-attractive tournaments are held one after another almost every week. Driving ranges are everywhere, and young and middle-aged men can often be seen on the streets practicing their swings with umbrella or just with their hands and arms alone. In a sense, all businessmen are more or less golfers. It is not unusual for important negotiations to be held on the green golf course rather than in their stuffy offices.

Volleyball

Among the various kinds of sports, volleyball is one of Japan's specialities. Even if measured by Olympic standards, both the Japanese men's and women's teams are of top grade. In 1964 when the Olympic Games were held in Tokyo, Japan's female team, known as the "Witches of the East," became the world champions, thus popularizing volleyball in Japan as a mass sport. Famous players on the all-Japan men's team are as popular as movie stars among teen-age girls, and countless amateur teams made up of housewives—commonly known as "mama-san volley"—can be seen everywhere in the country. Besides volleyball, soccer and basketball are also very popular.

Skiing

Skiing is another booming winter sport in Japan. Skiers can hardly wait for the snow season, which makes its first appearance in December in the northern sections of Japan. The full-fledged skiing season extends between January and March, a time when the Japanese National Railways operates many "ski special trains." Among the most popular skiing resorts near Tokyo are those in Gumma, Niigata and Nagano Prefectures. In a few places in the Tohoku and Hokkaido areas, one can even enjoy summer skiing.

Skating

Winter skating now attracts an enormous group of fashionable enthusiasts to natural skating rinks like the one in the Fuji Five Lakes and Karuizawa areas. Indoor rinks, some of which are seasonally converted from swimming pools, also attracts their share of the young skating enthusiasts.

"Pachinko"

"What do you do in your free time?" was among the questions asked in a recent national survey on ordinary recreation in Japan. The most frequent reply by men was "pachinko," or pinball game. It originated as a marble game for children, but today there is a sign at the door of pinball parlors, saying: "No one under 18 years old admitted." Millions of adults now enjoy "pachinko" as a practical combination of a hobby and a way to make profit. If luck is in your favor, your small steel balls can be exchanged for a wide variety of prizes of your choice, ranging from cigarettes to chocolate, from clothing to magazines. However, there is no cash payoff. "Pachinko" is thus the recreation of the common man.

Mahjong

Although mahjong originated in China, it is now more popular in Japan and is even rampant among college students. "Janso" is the name for the mahjong parlors that are ubiquitous in many campus towns and, surprisingly enough filled with students both day and night. For such students, mahjong could well be their college major. This betting game is so appealing that players are apt to forget all sense of time and sit up all night long without realizing it in what is known in Japanese as "tetsuman." Salaried men also like to play mahjong, and just as in the case of another rampant pastime—golfing, they sometimes discuss business matters while they play.

Horse Racing

Horse racing, one of the officially permitted gambling operations in Japan, is run either by the state or by local authorities. Among the 1,500 people polled by the Leisure Development Center in 1975, 20 percent expressed interest in horse racing and had actually bought pari-mutuel tickets. These tickets can be bought at the race track where the races are held or at off-course betting places set up in the busy sections of the city.

More than 145,900 people attended the 44th Japan Derby held in May 1977, making an all-time record for total sales for one day of 14,000 million yen.

"Go" Game

"Go" consists of a total of 361 black and white stones, of which 180 whites are used by the chief player and the remaining 181 blacks are played by his opponents. The stones are played alternately, one at a time, by placing them with a clicking sound on the intersection of 19 horizontal and 19 vertical lines painted on a square wooden board. When the board is filled up with stones, the player who occupies a larger territory (encircled by his stones) than his opponent's, is regarded as a winner.

"Shogi"

Often compared with Western-style chess, Japanese "shogi" also uses 40 chess pieces (20 to each player) and consists of tactical moves similar to those in chess. One of the main differences is that "kin" (gold) and "gin" (silver) pieces are not found in Western-style chess. The "kin" performs the duties of the queen, which is why no queen is necessary in "shogi." Another key difference is that captive pieces continue to be included in the opponent's tactics.

Hot Springs

Hot Springs A volcanic country, Japan is a true "mecca" of hotsprings enthusiasts. For many people traveling is synonymous with traveling to hot-spring resorts. Natural hot springs are regarded as efficacious for a wide variety of ailments such as neuralgia, gastroenteritis and sterility. As the older people are interested in hot-springs cures, there are some spas that specialize in providing this type of medical treatment. At such places, visitors sometimes stay as long as a month, doing their own daily cooking. In the cases of gastroenteric disorder, patients may drink a certain kind of hot mineral water while standing under falling hot-spring water so that it hits sore shoulders, aching back or painful waist.

Outdoor Hot Springs In Japan hot springs are apt to gush out almost any place—beside a river, on a beach or high up a mountain, thus providing a wide variety of

Sand bath   Outdoor hot springs

outdoor hot springs. This means that one can soak in a hot spring while enjoying the beauty of cherry blossoms in springtime or the autumn tints—a typical Japanese-style charm. Mixed bathing is not unusual at those outdoor hot springs.

Sand Baths The most famous sand bath is Surigahama Beach of Ibusuki Spa in Kagoshima Prefecture. On the beach is a natural hot springs, where the temperature of the water is moderated by mixing it with sea water. Just lie down on the beach, cover yourself with sand all over and you will soon feel comfortably warm.

"Hanami"

This literally means to watch or enjoy flowers, particularly when the cherry blossom season is in full swing, presenting a typical scene when the Japanese people carry out their inner belief that "dumpling rather than blossoms." Under the cherry blossoms they spread a picnic blanket, and the indispensable Japanese "sake" makes them sing, dance and sometimes go to excess. The best-known "hanami" place in Tokyo is Ueno Park between late March and early April. You have to get there earlier to find a good spot. "Hanami" is a typically Japanese-style spring recreation.

"Momiji-Gari"

Japan has long been said to offer the most spectacular autumn colors. When the frost falls late in October on the main island of Honshu, trees in the mountainous areas begin to present a natural masterpiece of brocade, with all the delicacies of hues from maple crimson to gingko yellow. This is the time when many people plan a "momiji-gari," or autumn-leaves viewing, to enjoy one of the most beautiful autumn seasons in the world. There is no "sake" or wild partying, contrary to the "hanami" (cherry-blossom viewing) season. Among the most ideal places for "momiji-gari" near Tokyo are Nikko and Hakone.

Mountaineering and Swimming Season

The official season for mountain climbing and sea bathing in Japan opens on July 1 and lasts for two months—July and August. At Mt. Fuji, for example, hundreds of climbers converge on Fuji-Yoshida at the foot of mountain on the eve of June 30. As soon as the opening ceremony is over at mid-night, they start climbing so that they can enjoy the sunrise from high up on the mountain. As September draws near, the mountain climate becomes quite changeable and the beaches are plagued by huge waves. It's the typhoon season and time for the summer season to officially close.

Mountaineering

The mountaineering population in Japan is constantly increasing. On weekend nights, terminal railway stations are full of young climbers bound for the Japan Alps and other mountains around the country. Some of them are bold enough to go mountain-climbing even if the weather forecast is quite unfavorable, and are sometimes criticized for their "kamikaze" climbing mentality. In fact, many alpine accidents are reported, particularly in the winter season. However, there was one brilliant accomplishment in 1975—International Ladies' Year—when a Japanese female mountaineering team successfully conquered the summit of Mt. Everest, marking the first time in history that women climbed the world's highest mountain.

Tokaido Natural Footpath

When the government announced its basic plan to make the Tokaido a natural footpath in January 1969, millions of nature lovers enthusiastically welcomed the new plan on the idea that once-lost nature could thus be retrieved from the violent hands of destructive bulldozers. In fact, they could hardly wait for its completion, and began walking along the nature paths called "shizen-hodo" while they were partly under construction. The footpath was completed three years later, and today the distance of 1,736 km. can be covered on foot from Mt. Takao on the western outskirts of Tokyo to Mino-o Park in Osaka.

Fishing

Fishing   Surrounded by the sea and with many rivers in the inland areas, Japan provided many ideal places for fishing. The number of anglers is estimated at over 10 million. Though the catch differs according to the district, they fish in the sea for bonito, red snapper, yellowtail, saurel, etc., and in the rivers for a variety of trout, char, "ayu" (sweetfish), pond smelt, etc. Fishing for "ayu", trout and char is restricted and the fishing season for each is fixed by regulations. The "ayu" season, for instance, opens at the beginning of June, and as soon as the first day dawns, many enthusiastic anglers head for the rivers and streams, wading deep up to their waist in their anxiety to catch their share of this sweet-tasting fish.

"Wakasagi" Fishing   "Wakasagi" (pond smelt) fishing is no doubt one of the most colorful winter pastimes. One makes a hole in the ice of a frozen lake and drops his fishing line into the water beneath the ice. This way of fishing is commonly seen at such places as Lake Yamanaka and Lake Kawaguchi, which are easily accessible from the Tokyo metropolitan area.

"Yana"   This is a way to catch "ayu" (sweetfish), and other river fish during the ideal season of early summer. This "yana"-style fishing widely prevails throughout most of the nation—from Honshu all the way down to Kyushu. At "yana" fishing sites, there are also riverside restaurants where one may enjoy dining on sweetfish fresh from the river. Their specialty is what is called an "ayu full course," consisting of "ayu" broiled with salt, "miso"-daubed bean curd and caramelized riverfish.

Cormorant Fishing   Cormorant fishing is a unique, traditional way of fishing that dates from the 8th century. Present-day cormorant fishing can best be observed on the Nagara River in Gifu Prefecture, where a group of skillful fishermen each control several trained cormorants on moonless summer nights. To ensure cormorants resist the temptation to swallow their "ayu" (sweetfish) catches, steel rings around their neck mercilessly prevent them from doing so. The entire demonstration can be observed from a pleasure boat floating down the same river, with such additional features as dinner on board and geisha entertainment. This style of fishing also practiced on the Oi River in Kyoto, the Mikuma River in Kyushu and the Hiji River on Shikoku Island.

Rapids Shooting

With the mountainous belt running down its center, the long and slender Japanese archipelago is characterized, among other things, by its many rapids. In fact, several rivers in Japan have a rapid current. It is a thrilling experience to shoot the rapids, as expert boatmen skillfully maneuver their flat-bottomed boats with only a single oar, avoiding rocks that jut up here and there along the way. Japanese rivers traditionally famous for providing an opportunity to shoot the rapids are the Tenryu, Hozu, Kiso and Mogami Rivers.

Rapid shooting

ENTERTAINMENT

Kabuki

Kabuki   Kabuki is one of Japan's traditional theatrical arts. The word kabuki is the applicable term for all of the classical and dramatic forms that gradually developed from a primitive "prayer dance" created toward the end of the 16th century by Okuni, a shrine maiden at the Great Shrine of Izumo. Ever since its infancy, kabuki has been popularly supported by the general public over the ensuing four centuries.

Kabuki plays may be classified into three groups—"jidaimono" (plays with historical themes), "sewamono" (genre-plays) and "kizewamono" (lit. true "sewamono").

157

The major dramatists who wrote the kabuki plays performed on the stage today were Monzaemon Chikamatsu (1653–1724), who turned out more than 100 dramatic love stories, and Mokuami Kawatake, whose realistic social dramas totaled more than 300.

Stage   Two outstanding features seen in the stage plan of kabuki drama are the "hanamichi" and "mawari-butai." "Hanamichi," or flower way, is an elevated passage leading to the stage through the audience, but which is in reality an extension of the stage where some important parts of plays are performed from time to time. "Mawari-butai" is equipped with a mechanism similar to a turntable. Known as a revolving stage, it is a device for the rapid shifting of scenes bringing into view a scene that has been readied behind stage.

"Uma-no-Ashi"   "Uma-no-ashi," or the front and back parts of a stage horse, is played by a couple of men to represent a horse. A live horse never appears on the kabuki stage. "Uma-no-ashi" perform on stage in a costume designed to resemble a horse without ever showing their faces. In other words, they are really unseen actors, although they need a series of excellent team work.

"Uma-no-ashi"

"Oyama"   In olden times when kabuki was still in the early stages of its development, it was felt that the appearance of actresses on the stage produced a demoralizing effect on the audience. As a result, it has been usual for actors to play the part of women. These actors, called "oyama" or "onnagata" (lit. form of women), even try to act like women in their daily life.

"Kumadori" "Kumadori" is another technical word used in kabuki drama meaning a special make-up style often used by an actor who plays the role of ruffian called "aragoto." The object is to intensify the emotions an actor wishes to convey to the audience.

Three of the typical make-up types seen on the stage are illustrated below.

"Kumadori"

"Kuroko" or "Kurogo" The "kuroko" corresponds to the prompter in Western-style drama. A "kuroko" is dressed and hooded in black to make himself as unobtrusive as possible; hence, the name "kuroko" (lit. black man). The job of a "kuroko," done by one of the assistants of the stage manager, is to aid the actors during a stage performance.

Noh

Noh Noh is a classical dance-drama based on a heroic subject, making use of chants and highly stylized, measured movements. In olden times noh was patronized by the nobility, while kabuki was supported by common people.

Noh performers consist of a "shite" (principal actor),

"waki" (secondary actor), "tsure" (associates) and "kyogen-kata" (noh comedians).

The noh orchestra is made up of a "taiko" (large drum), "otsuzumi" (medium-sized drum), "kotsuzumi" (small drum) and "fue" (flute) arranged to sit in the order mentioned, from left to right, as the audience faces the stage. The orchestra is accompanied by the recitative chants of "yokyoku" or "utai," which amounts to the libretto of a noh play.

Appreciation   The degree of one's aesthetic appreciation of noh plays depends on the sensitivity of each member of the audience observing the performance. In appreciating noh plays, some people are of the opinion that the performance should be observed from an "avant-garde" approach rather than with an attitude based on a classical perspective. It has the operatic character more than the dramatic one.

Noh plays performed overseas have usually had an enthusiastic response from audiences. A newspaper reported that the members of these foreign audiences reacted this way because they felt Japanese noh plays were the "in" thing to enjoy as part of the latest "avant-garde" movement.

Stage   The noh stage proper is 5.5 m. square, with four pillars and a wall at the back. It is a sort of roofed platform, or a "house within a house." This is the place where the acting is done. Half the size of the acting stage, it is where musicians perform. On the right of the stage is a one-meter-wide veranda, which seats the chorus. On the wall at the back of the stage is a painting of a pine tree, symbolic of the time when noh plays were performed outdoors on a lawn with pine trees as a background. The other three sides of the stage are open.

There are no stage sets in the noh play, except for a few plays in which a pine tree or a boat is used to suggest an entire scene.

Masks   Generally, the "shite" actor wears a mask, while no other actors are masked. To mask the face of the chief actor does not simply mean to cover his face, however. The actor concentrates his complete attention on wearing the mask in order to demonstrate something going on inside his mind while the noh play is being performed. Noh masks may be roughly classified into the following 16 types:

1. old men 2. old women 3. middle-aged women 4. middle-aged men 5. young men 6. young women 7. children 8. blind men 9. gentle gods 10. powerful gods 11. formidable gods 12. fairies 13. supernatural beings 14. monsters 15. demons 16. wild animals

Action   The action observed in noh plays, is classified into about 250 different forms called for in these plays. The action, represented in "mai" (dance), is not a type of dancing, but an elaborately stylized presentation of body movement aimed at impressing the inner consciousness.

Theaters   The principal theaters where noh is generally performed are as follows:

Ginza Nohgakudo	Ginza, Tokyo
Kanze Kaikan	Shibuya-ku, Tokyo
Kita Nohgakudo	Shinagawa-ku, Tokyo
Suidobashi Nohgakudo	Bunkyo-ku, Tokyo
Umewaka Nohgakudo	Nakano-ku, Tokyo
Kongo Nohgakudo	Muromachi, Kyoto
Kyoto Kanze Kaikan	Okazaki, Kyoto
Otsuki Nohgakudo	Higashi-ku, Osaka

There are also theaters for the performance of noh in Kobe,

Matsuyama, Kanazawa, Fukuoka and Otaru.

"Kyogen"

"Kyogen" are comic interludes performed to fill the intervals between noh plays. In striking contrast to modern comedy, "kyogen" features dialogue delivered in old-fashioned language that is no longer used in present-day Japan. But its humorous interludes are fully enjoyed by the audience.

"Kyogen" also has a secondary meaning in modern Japanese usage—a falsehood.

"Bunraku"

Ballads chanted by a minstrel to the accompaniment of "biwa" (Japanese lute) caught the fancy of the people in 13th-century Japan. This type of ballad came to be known as "joruri." And in later years, puppet element was added to "joruri," creating a sort of composite art now known as puppet drama, or "bunraku."

In puppet drama, the audience will find, across the stage near the front, a long panel about 45-cm. high, behind which the puppets are operated. This panel section serves to conceal the lower part of the operator's body.

Puppet dramas can be observed at the National Theater in Tokyo or at Asahi-za Theater in Osaka, although they are not performed on a regular basis. On a small island in the Inland Sea named Awaji-shima, one can enjoy puppet shows in the waiting room of the ferry.

"Shingeki"

A reactionary movement against kabuki was launched before World War I by an association of literary men headed by Shoyo Tsubouchi (1859–1935), professor of literature at Waseda University, who translated the complete works of William Shakespeare into Japanese. Since then a new type of drama—literally called "shingeki" (new drama)—emerged.

Among many works that have been staged by "shingeki" troupes are Chekhov's "The Cherry Orchard," Gorky's "The Lower Depths" and Tennessee Williams' "A Streetcar Named Desire." The Haiyu-za Theater (located in Roppongi, Minato-ku, Tokyo) is noted for its performances of "shingeki" dramas.

All-Girl Revues

All-Girl Revues   This form of theatrical art featuring girls playing both male as well as female parts got its start in 1913. These revues consist of a lively succession of dialogue, song and dance by a galaxy of well-trained girls accompanied by an orchestra usually playing Western music. Most of them are based on a sentimental, romantic story of love and friendship. The Takarazuka Girls Troupe, well-known for its scintillating performances, has enjoyed an excellent reputation among revue enthusiasts—mostly teen-age girls—since its performance began in 1913 with only 16 girls on stage. The troupe has now 377 members.

Takarazuka Girls Troupe   The Takarazuka Girls Troupe consists of unmarried girls performing "All-Girl Operas" on stage. "All-Girl Operas" is a magic name for young Japanese girls, and through them some of the magic even rubs off on the adult world. But this Japanese version of the opera is altogether different from Western-style opera. It is a combination of a light operetta and a revue, and the performers are girls in their late teens and their 20's. When these girls get married, they have to resign from the troupe. The troupe is familiarly called the "Takarazuka School," with a growing number of actresses appearing from among the graduates of the "school."

Shochiku Opera Troupe   This troupe was once featured as an all-girl's opera in the same way as the Takarazuka Girls Troupe. Recently, however, it dropped the word "girls" from its troupe name and is now active in performing lavish chorus-line dances staged at the Kokusai Theater in Asakusa, Tokyo. Its performances feature a series of "odori" (dance) throughout the year to conform to the season—Natsu-no Odori (Summer Dance), Aki-no Odori (Autumn Dance), etc.

Movies

Japan is now one of the foremost movie-producing nations of the world. Its so-called "Big Four" movie companies (Nikkatsu, Shochiku, Toei and Toho) and other minor independent studios produce more than 200 films a year, which are shown in 2,600 movie theaters throughout the country. Films for adults only are increasing in number, with critics vigorously debating films featuring gangsters called "yakuza," pornographic effects and similar controversial themes.

Besides these films, more than 200 films are annually imported. About 185 million customers enjoy both the Japanese and foreign films every year, with annual box-office receipts amounting to 14,000 million yen. Admission fees to movie theaters range from ¥800 to ¥2,000.

Symphony Orchestras

The NHK Symphony Orchestra, one of the seven major orchestras in Tokyo, is widely accepted as the finest performing orchestra. With a history dating back half a century, the NHK Symphony Orchestra belongs to the Japan National Broadcasting Corporation (NHK). Most of the concerts are held under the baton of such honored conductors of the orchestra as Wolfgang Sawallish, Otmar Suitner, Robro von Matačič, Holst Stein and other guest conductors from around the world. Its subscription concerts are performed six times a month.

Besides this orchestra, the New Japan Philharmonic Orchestra with its world-famous conductor, Seiji Ozawa, is especially popular among the young people.

In other major cities than Tokyo, there are also good orchestras managed by local public entities or broadcasting companies.

Noh play

TRANSPORTATION

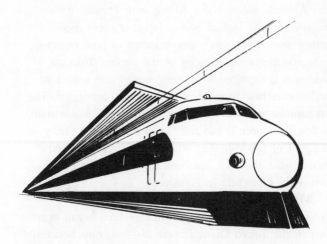

Shinkansen

The JNR (Japanese National Railways) Shinkansen superexpress train made its debut in October 1964 just in time for the Tokyo Olympiad. The computerized CTC (Central Train Control), installed at the headquarters in Tokyo, is responsible for the entire operation. Even unmanned control is now regarded as theoretically feasible. Running a maximum speed of 210 kph, 8 to 9 trains in an hour, the "Hikari" and "Kodama," leave from both ends—frequently enough to serve the thousands of passengers traveling every day. The Shinkansen service has gradually extended to the west—to Okayama in March 1972 and to Fukuoka in March 1975. The fastest "Hikari" train can cover the distance of 1.100 km. in 6 hours and 56 minutes.

Linear Motor Train

What's the next step after the Shinkansen superexpress train? A linear motor train! Along with France, West Germany and the United States, Japan is also experimenting with this entirely new concept of land transport. As the transportation capacity of the present Tokaido Shinkansen is expected to become inadequate sooner or later, another new form of train service is demanded. The most promise seems to be offered by the linear motor train, which will connect Tokyo and Osaka non-stop in one hour at a speed of 500 kph. The scheme has already moved forward, since the JNR has built an experimental track in Miyazaki Prefecture in Kyushu.

Monorail

Japan's longest, commercial monorail, which began operations in the Tokyo Olympic year of 1964, runs between Hamamatsu-cho and Tokyo International Airport. It has a maximum speed of 75–80 kph. and covers the distance of 13.1 km. in 15 min. You will find the Tokyo monorail astride an elevated ferroconcrete track, while Japan's second-largest monorail line, the Shonan monorail, runs between Ofuna and Enoshima near Kamakura, with the cars running along the concrete track hanging down like gondolas. The subway system built in Sapporo in time for the Winter Olympiad of 1972 is also a type of "best-riding monorail," which with its rubber tires runs comparatively free from the mechanical noises peculiar to ordinary subway trains.

A dual-purpose coach: daytime (left) at night (right)

Dual-Purpose Coach

In October 1967, a dual-purpose coach made its debut in
JNR's electric train service and is now widely used in
long-distance limited express train, such as the ones running between Tokyo and Aomori to the north, and Osaka
and Kagoshima to the south. It is regarded as a dual-
purpose coach because its ordinary, daytime seats can be
converted into sleeper berths at night—another JNR
example of rationalizing otherwise wasteful facilities.

Sleeper Coaches

There are two different types of sleeper coaches—the A-type
equivalent to first class and B-type second class. The B-type
sleepers are available either on the locomotive-powered
trains or on the more prevalent regular electric trains. The
sleeper coaches of the electric trains are either two or
three-berth sleepers. Unique among sleeper accommoda-
tions is an A-grade compartment, which is available only

SLEEPERS	TYPE OF COACHES	TIERS	WIDTH	LENGTH	SPACE BETWEEN TIRES
A type	Loco-hauled	upper	101 cm	193 cm	92 cm
		lower	101	193	113 cm
B type (for limited Express)	Loco-hauled (3-tier system)	upper	70	195	79
		middle	70	195	75
		lower	70	195	73
	Electric train	upper	70	190	68
		middle	70	190	68
		lower	106	190	76
	Loco-hauled (2-tier system)	upper	70	195	103
		middle	70	195	103

on the limited-express train "Asakaze" linking Tokyo and Fukuoka.

Train Telephone Service

Telephone service is available from all of the Tokyo-Hakata (Fukuoka) Shinkansen superexpress trains to the cities and towns scattered along the line, and vice versa. The system is fully automated and no switchboard operator is used. You can also call anywhere inside Japan from aboard a Seikan ferry boat traveling between Aomori and Hakodate, although only one-way traffic service is available.

Air-Conditioned Commuter Trains

Just imagine all the stifling heat and humidity of summer and coaches packed to three times normal capacity. Japanese commuter trains in summer are simply unbearable. To help ease this routine ordeal, air-conditioned trains have been added to railway service since 1967. Actually, they are not all air-conditioned yet, and you are quite lucky if you happen to catch one. The Chuo Line, one of the most crowded trains operating between Tokyo and Takao (53.1 km.), for instance, is air-conditioned about 30%, putting your chances of catching one at one out of three.

Since many commuters these days are apt to wait for the cool trains, riding in an air-conditioned train does not necessarily guarantee the summer comfort one might expect.

"Green Car"

Instead of the former system of offering first and second-class cars, the Japanese National Railways supposedly adopted a single-class system in 1969. The only thing is they didn't get rid of all the former first-class coaches—they simply renamed them "green cars," identifying them with green cloverleaf signs (cf. illustration). In this sense, the "green cars" are for all intents and purposes the second generation of the old first-class coaches. To ride in a "green car," therefore, one must purchase a "green car ticket" in addition to a regular ticket.

A "green car" symbol

A "green window" sign

"Green Window"

This is where you purchase special JNR tickets for limited express, sleeper and reserved-seat trains. They can be identified by the green sign (cf. illustration) at most of the major JNR stations as well as at the offices of the Japan Travel Bureau and other leading travel agencies. The great majority of these tickets are put on sale at 9 a.m. one week before the boarding date, and are controlled by a nation-wide on-line computer system. Despite the high-speed motorization age, train travel still remains predominant in Japan and every single ticket is often sold out right away for those convenient trains during the tourist seasons.

Automatic Ticket Vending Machines

In almost every case when you want to buy a train ticket on a national or private line costing up to ¥450, some ¥10, ¥50 and/or ¥100 coins are really indispensable. This is because your ticket sellers are now, with few exceptions, automatic vending machines. Of course, they return any change left over. When you are out of coins, you may either get change from a station employee or break your ¥1,000 note by inserting it into an automatic exchange machine and receiving the change in ¥100 coins.

Station Platform Tickets

In contrast to the customs in some foreign countries, we are supposed to purchase a special ticket to gain entry onto station platforms. The only exception is at unmanned stations. "I don't intend to take the train myself, I just want to see my friend off." This excuse won't work. You simply won't be allowed to pass through the wicket without a station platform ticket.

Coloring of JNR Electric Trains

In the metropolitan Tokyo area there are many different JNR electric lines. Too confusing? Not really, since the trains of each line are brilliantly colored both for decoration and identification—light green for the Yamanote Line, orange for the Chuo Line, yellow for the Sobu Line and blue for the Keihin-Tohoku Line. Remember the color of your train and you will never get confused.

Train Diagram

The Japanese National Railways have long been proud of what they claim is the world's most punctual schedule. But will this be only a fond memory in the future? During the rush hours, they operate their commuter train runs rather acrobatically on an electronic diagram at the slim interval of two minutes. Take another example of such main trunk lines as the Tohoku, Shinetsu and Joetsu Lines. More and more limited express trains have been brought into service, and they, too, are operated on an ever-tighter schedule. Each train must go on the split-second diagram to avoid a rear-end collision. If you look at the diagram of any given train, you will find that that particular train is expected to pass such-and-such a station at exactly 21 minutes and 15 seconds after 14 o'clock. It is a matter of seconds.

Subway Service

Once the most popular means of surface transportation for the general public, the municipal streetcar has all but been abolished throughout the country because of its increasing inefficiency amid almost hopeless road conditions. In Tokyo alone, there are only two lines left covering a total of 13 km. in contrast to the golden age of the streetcar when as many as 41 lines covered no less than 352 km. Instead, the subway is now replacing it. Since its inauguration between Ueno and Asakusa on December 30, 1927, the subway network has continued to expand until today there are eight lines spread over a total distance of 160 km. There are subways in Osaka, Nagoya, Yokohama and Sapporo, with others under construction in Kyoto and Fukuoka.

Steam Locomotives

Steam locomotives (SL) finally disappeared from the

everyday scene at the end of 1975, after having played many a dramatic role in the century-long history of Japanese railways which was inaugurated in 1872 with the opening of a line between Shimbashi and Yokohama. Many ardent SL fans were so reluctant to bid farewell to the old locomotives that they have now created an "SL boom," taking photographs or recording the dynamic engine sounds. Main types of SL trains, all retired years ago, are being carefully maintained in their original state at the Umekoji Maintenance Center near Kyoto Station.

The Transportation Museum in Tokyo exhibits Japan's first SL of British make and the historical "Benkei-goh," which ran for the first time in Hokkaido.

SL Hotels

This is apparently a spin-off from the "SL boom." Retired steam locomotives together with several coaches were obtained and converted into commercial hotels. An SL hotel is open for business in Nakamura, Kochi Prefecture, another in Nobeyama, Nagano Prefecture, in Fukagawa, Hokkaido and in Okinawa Prefecture.

"Ozashiki Ressha"

"Ozashiki ressha," or banquet room train, is another fashionable variation of JNR's recent series of innovations. JNR was shrewed enough to incorporate all the trappings of a Japanese-style banquet room including "tatami" and paper screens, in an otherwise ordinary carriage so that passengers may relax and enjoy themselves in traditional Japanese surroundings, even during a train ride. The "ozashiki ressha" is primarily available for special trains chartered by large groups.

Taxies

The best place to find a taxi in Japan is at the taxi stands located near most railways stations, although one can also catch any empty, cruising cab. When one stops for you, it's not necessary to open the door yourself, it's automatically controlled by the driver. There are, of course, hundreds of commercial taxi companies in any of the big cities, but private taxies are also available. Since December 1959, the coveted taxi license has been given only to skillful, reliable drivers of long standing—the main reason why many customers prefer private taxies.

Bus

City buses are now on mostly one-man-operations. In this conductorless system, you are supposed to pay yourself by dropping the required fare in the coin box beside the driver's seat when you get on the bus. Particularly in the big cities, public bus service suffers badly from serious traffic congestion every Monday through Friday. An experimental system is now under way to restrict the extreme left lane to buses during the morning rush hours between 7:00 and 9:00 o'clock. Signs are posted on these main roads reading "Smooth operation is our duty." Many local municipalities also operate their own public bus services, but many of them suffer from chronic financial difficulties, mainly due to operational inefficiency and rising costs.

Mini Shuttle Bus

City traffic is turning from bad to worse, and even beyond that stage in Tokyo. It is very difficult to find any ultimate solution, but one effective policy is to decrease the total number of individual cars driving in and out of the central part of the city. Since February 1974, the Tokyo Metropolitan Government has been operating a so-called "mini shuttle bus" service between Tokyo Central Station and Shimbashi Station via the Kasumigaseki government-office district. This shuttle bus service was inaugurated to encourage government officials to take the lead in giving up the use of their otherwise comfortable private cars. The mini bus has, therefore, been designed with a plush interior, including an air-conditioner, making the fare comparatively more expensive.

Expressway Buses

Long-distance buses operate the Tomei Expressway between Tokyo and Nagoya (366 km.) and the Meishin Expressway between Nagoya and Kobe (216 km.) at the comfortable maximum speed of 100 kph. At night, non-stop bus service is available from Tokyo to Nagoya, Kyoto, Osaka and Kobe, respectively, advertised by the unique slogan, "Dream-goh." One can also take an expressway bus to such tourist resorts as Hakone, the Fuji Five Lakes district and even the Fifth Station of Mt. Fuji (except in winter). Many tourists sometimes prefer these expressway buses because they can enjoy a close and better view of the scenery.

Carferry

A comparatively new means of transportation in Japan, carferry service is especially welcomed by young people, including honeymooners. Though business has become rather shaky these days with the emphasis on saving energy, there are still dozens of different routes serving various parts of the country, particularly starting from such big cities as Tokyo, Nagoya and Osaka. Here is a sample of one such route: From Kawasaki near Tokyo, one can take a luxurious carferry down to Hyuga near Miyazaki, Kyushu in about 20 hrs. A deluxe special-class cabin costs ¥26,400 per person plus ¥31,500 for transporting the car. Of course one can take a trip on a carferry without a car.

New Tokyo International Airport

Many of the world's famous airports have their own special reputation, including Tokyo International Airport at Haneda, which is the "world's most crowded airport." To cope with the increasingly busy jet-age traffic, the construction of another new international airport at Narita, some 68 km. east of Tokyo in Chiba Prefecture, was decided in 1967, with its official opening originally scheduled for 1971. The airport opened as an international airport in March 1978 after many local problems were solved.

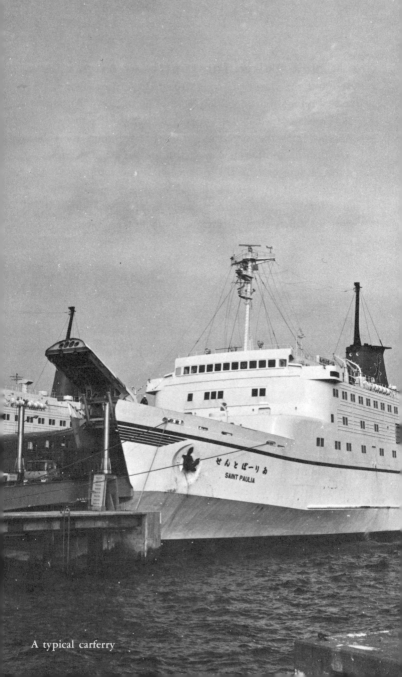
せんとぽーりあ
SAINT PAULIA

A typical carferry

SUPPLEMENT

All data, unless otherwise mentioned,
are based on those as of October 1977.

Population

Total Population: 112,145,133 (55,349,560 males and 56,795,573 females)

Source: National Census taken by the Ministry of Home Affairs.
Figures in parenthesis indicate the population of Tokyo Metropolis.

Population in Major Cities: .

Sapporo	1,255,658
Sendai	608,531
Tokyo	11,372,799 (8,323,395)
Yokohama	2,651,174
Nagoya	2,076,130
Kyoto	1,449,575
Osaka	2,655,026
Kobe	1,337,362
Hiroshima	844,022
Fukuoka	981,304

Number of Inbound and Outbound Travelers:

Source: Ministry of Transport.

Years	Inbound	Percentage over previous year	Outbound	Percentage over previous year
1971	660,715	—	961,135	—
1972	723,744	1.09	1,392,045	1.4
1973	784,691	1.08	2,288,966	1.4
1974	764,246	0.97	2,335,530	1.6
1975	811,072	1.06	2,466,326	1.1
1976	914,772	1.12	2,852,584	1.2

Climate

Temperature (in Centigrade):

	Winter (Jan.)	Spring (Apr.)	Summer (July)	Autumn (Oct.)	Annual Average
Asahikawa	− 8.3	4.5	20.4	8.5	6.2
Sapporo	− 5.1	6.1	20.2	10.4	7.8
Sendai	0.6	9.6	22.1	14.0	11.6
Tokyo	4.1	13.5	25.2	16.9	15.0
Nagoya	3.2	13.1	25.7	16.6	14.7
Kyoto	3.5	13.1	26.1	16.7	14.8
Osaka	4.5	13.9	26.8	17.6	15.6
Kobe	4.5	13.6	25.8	17.7	15.5
Hiroshima	4.1	13.0	25.5	16.8	14.8
Fukuoka	5.3	13.9	26.5	17.3	15.7
Kagoshima	6.7	15.6	26.9	19.1	17.0
Naha	16.0	20.8	28.2	24.1	22.3

Rainfalls and Humidity (Rainfalls in Millimeters):

	Winter (Jan.)	Spring (Apr.)	Summer (July)	Autumn (Oct.)	Annual Total Average
Asahikawa	81(82)	58(71)	119(79)	105(81)	1,159(79)
Sapporo	118(68)	104(75)	64(80)	90(74)	1,141(74)
Sendai	42(67)	132(71)	85(86)	170(77)	1,245(75)
Tokyo	49(66)	203(57)	122(79)	203(57)	1,503(69)
Nagoya	52(71)	136(69)	187(81)	133(76)	1,540(74)
Kyoto	56(67)	122(72)	145(76)	239(74)	1,638(73)
Osaka	50(68)	128(67)	181(75)	115(72)	1,390(71)
Kobe	46(63)	125(64)	191(77)	109(68)	1,367(77)
Hiroshima	51(71)	111(71)	156(82)	276(75)	1,644(75)
Fukuoka	77(74)	100(69)	134(80)	252(76)	1,705(75)
Kagoshima	91(75)	235(76)	347(82)	107(75)	2,433(77)
Naha	122(79)	149(70)	142(82)	174(74)	2,118(78)

(Figures in parentheses indicate humidity percentage)

The National Diet, Political Parties and Cabinet:

The Diet   The Diet consists of two Houses, the House of Representatives and the House of Councillors. Both Houses must resolve or approve, in principle, all legislative measures as well as the national budgets, the ratification of treaties, etc.

Political Parties   The major political parties are the Liberal-Democratic Party, the Japan Socialistic Party, the Komeito, the Japan Communist Party and the Democratic Socialist Party and New Liberal Club.

The strength of each of these parties and others in both Houses of the Diet as of July 1977 is:

Political Party	House of Representatives	House of Councillors
Liberal-Democratic (LDP)	259	124
Japan Socialist (JSP)	123	55
Komeito	56	16
Democratic Socialist (DSP)	28	28
Japan Communist (JCP)	19	11
New Liberal Club (NLC)	18	5
Niin Club	—	5
Minor	3	—
Independents	3	5
Vacant	2	3
Total number of seats	511	252

Cabinet   The Cabinet consists of the Prime Minister and 19 Cabinet Ministers. The Prime Minister is designated by the Cabinet and must himself or herself be a member of the Diet. The Prime Minister has the right to appoint or dismiss a Cabinet Minister.

Voting Rights   Any Japanese people 20 years of age or over, whether male or female has the right to vote in Diet elections as well as in prefectural and other elections.

The Legal (National) Holidays:

The Japanese nation observes the following 12 national holidays (if a holiday falls on a Sunday, the following day is treated as a holiday).

Jan. 1:   "Ganzitsu" or New Year's Day.

Jan. 15: "Seijin-no-Hi" or Adults' Day. This is the day
          dedicated to the nation's youths aged 20.

Feb. 11: "Kenkoku Kinen-no-Hi" or National Founda-
          tion Day.

Mar. 21: "Shumbun-no-Hi" or Vernal Equinox Day. This
or 22   day is set apart to promote the love of nature
          and all creatures, who are a part of it.

Apr. 29: "Tenno Tanjo-Bi" or the Emperor's Birthday.

May 3:   "Kempo Kinen-Bi" or Constitution Memorial
          Day.

May 5:   "Kodomo-no-Hi" or Children's Day or Boys'
          Festival.

Sept. 15: "Keiro-no-Hi" or Respect for the Aged Day.

Sept. 23: "Shubun-no-Hi" or Autumnal Equinox Day.
or 24   This day is set apart for ancestor worship.

Oct. 10: "Taiiku-no-Hi" or Sports Day.

Nov. 3:   "Bunka-no-Hi" or Culture Day. This day is set
          aside to foster the love of freedom and peace as
          well as the advancement of culture.

Nov. 23: "Kinro Kansha-no-Hi" or Labor Thanksgiving
          Day.

It is customarily regarded (although not legally designated) that the two con-
secutive days from January 2 are holidays. Offices and almost all shops are
usually closed on those days.

    In some rural districts, annual functions are observed according to the lunar
calendar. As a result, the New Year holidays generally come during the first half
of February.

National Parks

(From north to south)

Location: Hokkaido

1. Rishiri-Rebun-Sarobetsu
2. Shiretoko
3. Akan
4. Daisetsuzan
5. Shikotsu-Toya

Location: Honshu

6. Towada-Hachimantai
7. Rikuchu-Kaigan (Coast)
8. Bandai-Asahi
9. Nikko
10. Joshinetsu-Kogen (Plateau)
11. Chichibu-Tama
12. Ogasawara Islands (1,000 km. from Tokyo)
13. Fuji-Hakone-Izu
14. Chubu Sangaku (Mountain)
15. Minami (Southern) Alps
16. Hakusan
17. Ise-Shima
18. Yoshino-Kumano

19. San-in Kaigan (Coast)
20. Daisen-Oki
21. Seto-Naikai (Inland Sea) Part of Shikoku, Kyushu
22. Ashizuri-Uwakai Part of Shikoku

Location: Kyushu

23. Aso
24. Unzen-Amakusa
25. Saikai
26. Kirishima-Yaku
27. Iriomote

Besides the above there are 50 Quasi-National Parks.

Industrial Output

Source: The Ministry of International Trade and Industry
Figures in parenthesis indicate those exported.

Camera	Unit: Million	Timepieces	Unit: Ten million
1974	664	1974	688
1975	732	1975	568
1976	813	1976	709

Automobile	Source: National Census taken by the Automobile Industry Assoc.
1973	4,471,000 (1,450,000)
1974	3,932,000 (1,727,000)
1975	4,569,000 (1,827,000)

Figures of the largest, the highest and the longest items:

The largest lake	Lake Biwa in Kansai, Honshu, 235 km. in circumference, 674 sq. km. in area.
The deepest lake	Lake Tazawa in Tohoku, Honshu, 423 m. in depth.
The longest river	The Shinano River in Chubu, Honshu, 367 km. in length.
The longest bridge	Fujigawa Bridge in Chubu, Honshu, 1,373 m. in length.
The longest tunnel	The Ena Tunnel in Chubu, Honshu, 8,489 m. in length.
The highest mountain	Mt. Fuji in Chubu, Honshu, 3,776 m. in height.
The highest building	"Sunshine 60" Bldg. in Ikebukuro, Tokyo, 240 m. in height.

INDEX

A BIRD'S-EYE VIEW OF JAPAN
〈日本よもやま話〉

1976年5月10日　初版発行
1979年4月1日　改訂3版
(April 1, 1979 3rd edition)

定価 990円
（送料実費共145円）

編集人　広 木 昌 人
発行人　宮 越 茂 夫
発行所　日本交通公社
出版事業局

東京都千代田区神田鍛冶町3－3
大木ビル8階（〒101）
電話 編集部直通　03-257-8369
販売係 〃　03-257-8325
振替番号　東京 0-29403

印刷所　交通印刷株式会社
東京都新宿区東五軒町35

（53—284）

2026—2403—5847